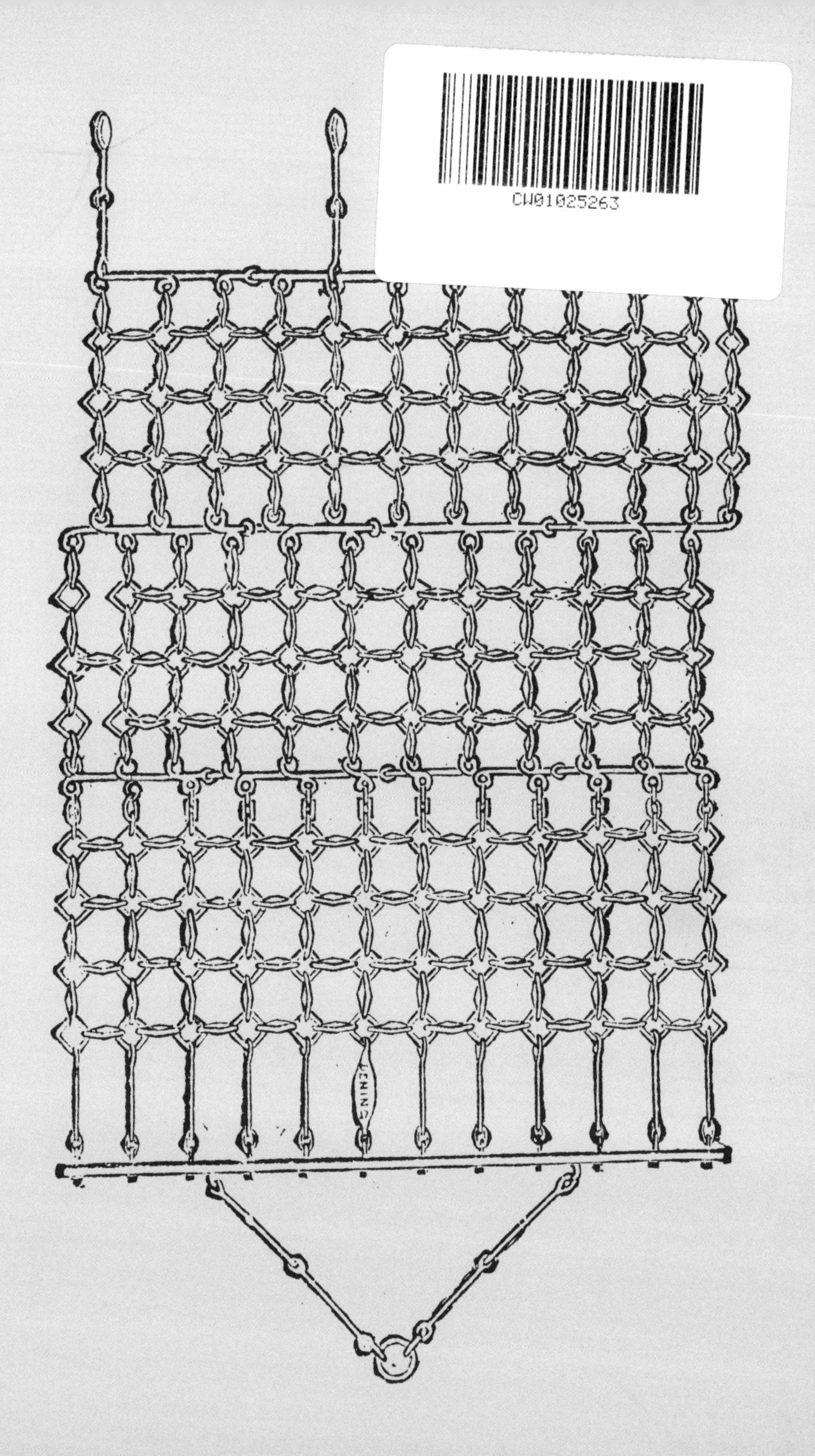
LENINS

The Old Words *of*
Herefordshire

Old Man, or Lad's-Love, – in the name there's nothing
To one that knows not Lad's-Love, or Old Man,
The hoar-green feathery herb, almost a tree,
Growing with rosemary and lavender.
Even to one that knows it well, the names
Half decorate, half perplex, the thing it is:
At least, what that is clings not to names
In spite of time. And yet I like the names.

from 'Old Man' by EDWARD THOMAS

The Old Words *of* Herefordshire

Edited by

Richard Wheeler

LOGASTON PRESS

ILLUSTRATIONS, INCLUDING ENDPAPERS, TAKEN FROM: **Walter J. Malden,** ***Tillage and Implements*** **(Bell's Agricultural Series),** George Bell & Sons, 1891

First published 2024 by Logaston Press
The Holme, Church Road, Eardisley HR3 6NJ
www.logastonpress.co.uk
An imprint of Fircone Books Ltd.

ISBN 978-1-910839-76-8

Designed & typeset by Richard Wheeler in 10.5 on 15 Caslon.
Cover design by Richard Wheeler.

Printed & bound in the Czech Republic.

Logaston Press is committed to a sustainable future for our business, our readers and our planet. The book in your hands is made from paper certified by the Forest Stewardship Council.

British Library Catalogue in Publishing Data.
A CIP catalogue record for this book is available from the British Library.

CONTENTS

ACKNOWLEDGEMENTS vii

PREFACE ix

INTRODUCTION 1

THE GLOSSARY 17

Local names of birds in Herefordshire 175

Calls to animals 177

Waggoners' calls 178

BIBLIOGRAPHY 179

for Jesse
with all my love

ACKNOWLEDGEMENTS

This book draws on the work of several earlier writers who compiled glossaries of Herefordshire dialect words. In particular: John Duncumb (1765–1839), George Cornewall Lewis (1806–63), Francis Tebbs Havergal (1829–90), Winifred Leeds (1883–1984) and Andrew Haggard (1892–1976). A major source of inspiration for this book has been the advocacy for place-language of Robert Macfarlane, nowhere more richly articulated than in his 2015 book, *Landmarks*.

I would like to thank Professor David Crystal for kindly agreeing to read the manuscript and provide comments; Bill Fleming, for his interest in this project and for generously sharing some observations on local dialect, from 'a lifetime of listening closely to people, lived largely in Herefordshire'; and Tony Waldis of the Tools and Trades History Society, for his help and advice. Finally, thank you to Su for your patience and support.

Oh that my words were now written!
Oh that they were printed in a book.

JOB 23

The difference between the almost-right word and the right word is really a large matter – it's the difference between the lightning-bug and the lightning.

MARK TWAIN

What words say does not last. The words last.
Because words are always the same,
and what they say is never the same.

ANTONIO PORCHIA

Words are all we have.

SAMUEL BECKETT

PREFACE

Words come and go. As we change, so too the words we use to tell of the world we inhabit. This turnover is natural. While new words are coined, others slip from sight and sound. In these pages are more than 3,000 words and phrases once spoken or written by people in Herefordshire. They come from a variety of sources, including word-lists compiled in the nineteenth and twentieth centuries. Such words can seem like *dwarf money* turned up by the blade of a plough. But this is not archaeology and these words are not lifeless artefacts. They still have things to say. Many things, but two things in particular.

Firstly, the act of naming is an act of seeing. In a fundamental way, naming confers visibility. We are more likely to notice and register the type of suspended hurdle used to stop cattle wandering up a stream if we know its name: *argy* (from the Welsh *ar Gwy*: 'on Wye'). This bond between naming and seeing has never been more vital. Has the world – the natural world, the environment – ever been in greater need of our attentiveness? Yet this at a time when threats to that attentiveness have never been more numerous or profound. Surely the need to treasure words as ways to connect with the world has never been more urgent.

Secondly, the local words we use, the local names we give to things, speak of a particular set of interactions with that place. Not of anywhere, but of here. Of what is specific to *this* place. As communications and travel have expanded, so too the range and scope of our outlook. The actual village gives way to the global village. There is much to celebrate in this. But one corollary is a spreading uniformity and the loss of the local. This can be seen in vernacular architecture, once infinitely richer in its vocabulary of local building materials and modes of construction. And the same can be said of language.

And yet the old words endure. They can still be found if we look for them. Spoken again, they might be heard again. And if so, we might recover a little of the local we have lost – and all the riches that might attend such a recovery.

RW, MARCH 2024

INTRODUCTION

THE 3,000 traditional dialect words contained in this glossary comprise just some – and probably just a small fraction – of those lost from everyday use in Herefordshire during the last two-plus centuries. They are drawn from a number of sources, including a variety of dialect word-lists for the county compiled between 1804 and 1974, together with other non-lexical and local sources.

Before exploring some of these in more detail, it is important first to consider what is meant by a dialect word, and in particular a *Herefordshire* dialect word. In essence, dialect refers to variations in language, and specifically to variations in vocabulary, pronunciation and grammar. (Accents also play a key role in linguistic variation, but as a speaker can give voice to a dialect from one region in the accent of another, dialect and accent are more usefully considered as distinct entities).

That language varies across the country seems self-evident. But mapping these variations is an elusive pursuit. Words live mercurial lives and dialects are not crisply demarcated one from another in terms of place; rather they form a continuum. As the sociolinguist Peter Trudgill puts it:

> Dialects differ from immediately neighbouring dialects only slightly, and can be heard to change slowly and word by word, pronunciation by pronunciation, as you travel from one village to the next.
>
> *The Dialects of England*, 1990

This being so, for convenience dialectologists *do* draw lines on maps in places 'most closely resembling an abrupt transition' (ibid). Unsurprisingly, such transitions do not coincide with county boundaries. A *Herefordshire* dialect word, then, is a word used in Herefordshire, but not necessarily *only* in Herefordshire.

In a pattern replicated nationwide, dialect words recorded in Herefordshire range from words whose use may indeed have been restricted to the county, or even to a locale or individual settlement, through to words that had far wider geographical currency (constituting the majority of dialect words found in the county). In the former category might be the word *arc*, as precisely defined and attributed by Francis Havergal in a Herefordshire glossary of 1887:

> Arc = a peculiar cloud or cirrus across the sky, N. to S., seen in the morning and evening only on rare occasions. It is said to be 'pointed, bright at the ends, and very pretty.' I have found this word only in a low damp part of Upton Bishop among very old people.

The latter category, for example, would include such words as *barm* (from the Anglo-Saxon *beorma*, meaning yeast). This has been recorded not only in Herefordshire but many other parts of the country, including in the far north.

In the nineteenth century, the recording of dialect words was essentially a haphazard and unmethodical activity carried out by compilers of varying backgrounds and expertise. The work entailed visiting communities and interviewing dialect speakers in order to glean words, phrases and definitions. Even today, with sociolinguistics a well-established field of academic research, to carry out such an exercise in a way that might be considered methodical or comprehensive would be extremely challenging.

Nonetheless, diligent efforts have sporadically been made to transcribe the dialect words of Herefordshire. And while the limitations and inconsistencies of these word-lists should be acknowledged, the work of their compilers should be celebrated. The earliest of these was John Duncumb, and without him and those who followed, words that might otherwise have been lost, live on.

John Duncumb (1765–1839)

In 1804, historian and topographer John Duncumb compiled a short glossary of 'Provincial Words and Phrases' for Herefordshire. Having moved to the county in 1788, Duncumb edited the *Hereford Journal* for three years, and was the first secretary of the Herefordshire Agricultural Society. However, he is best known for his unfinished *Collections towards the History and Antiquity of Hereford*, commissioned by Charles Howard, 11th duke of Norfolk, who held extensive estates in the county. The first volume was published in 1804, and it was here that his glossary first appeared.

Duncumb's glossary is a short one, with just 108 entries and most of the definitions limited to a few words: '*Beethy*, withered ... *Gorstly*, abounding in furze' etc. Nonetheless, it represents the first attempt to gather together and publish dialect words then in use in the county. It also represents, not just for Herefordshire but more widely, an early instance of a recognition of dialect's potential for an understanding of place.

George Cornewall Lewis (1806–63)

In the year of Duncumb's death, 1839, a far more comprehensive glossary appeared, both in terms of the number of entries (around 700) and the detail of its definitions. *A Glossary of Provincial Words used in Herefordshire and some of the Adjoining Counties* was compiled by George Cornewall Lewis, 'with the assistance of gentlemen resident in various parts of Herefordshire'. Lewis's country seat, Harpton Court, stood just over the Herefordshire border near Old Radnor (before being mostly demolished in 1956). His glossary sought to address the shortcomings, as he saw them, of Duncumb's list, which he criticised as 'meager and imperfect', and accessible only within the pages of 'a scarce and expensive book'.

Lewis is a contradictory figure. While his interests and talents lay in the study of languages and ancient history, he gave much of his time to a political career for which he had no obvious appetite and was arguably ill-equipped. He won entry to Parliament only when standing uncontested and was apparently a hopeless orator, yet held the posts of Chancellor of the Exchequer during the Crimean War, as well as Home Secretary.

There are inconsistencies too in his assertions about dialect use. In his preface to the *Glossary*, he claims that: 'A provincial word seems properly to mean a word which is not actually used in the written or spoken language of educated persons'. And yet this highly-educated gentleman made ready use of dialect words in his correspondence with others of his circle. (As further evidence of his appetite for words, Lewis appears to have coined the extraordinary adjective 'venisonivorous' to describe those with a predilection for venison. His use of the word in a letter of 1831 is noted in the *Oxford English Dictionary* as the only known instance of the word in written English.)

Lewis's *Glossary* makes plain his wide-ranging knowledge, not only of the local dialect but others from across the country, together with their written sources. His entry for *beethy* (compare with Duncumb's) is typical:

> **Beethy**, *adj.* soft, sticky, contrary to crisp, overripe. It is also said of a person in a slight perspiration. Grose in *v.* states that underdone meat is so called in Herefordshire; but this sense is not known at present. In Boucher's Glossary, to *beath* is explained to mean 'to dry by exposure to the fire.' To *bathe* is used by Chaucer, as equivalent to *bask*. From these uses it may be inferred that *beethy* means such a degree of moisture as is created in a porous substance by imperfect exposure to heat, sufficient to cause the steam to pervade it, but not drive it off entirely.

The 1820s and 1830s saw a marked growth in the study and publication of English dialects. Local glossaries appeared for Suffolk (1823), Somerset (1825), Cheshire (1826), Yorkshire (1828), East Anglia (1830), Sussex (1836) and Devon (1837). Early stabs were also made at dialect dictionaries of national scope, with the publication of Boucher's *A Glossary of Obsolete and Provincial Words Forming a Supplement to the Dictionaries of the English Language* in 1833, and Grose's *A Glossary of Provincial and Local Words used in England* in 1839.

In 1873 the English Dialect Society was founded by the philologist Walter Skeat, and in the two decades before its winding up in 1896, dozens more glossaries appeared. Following the pattern established in the first half of the nineteenth century, these were typically county or part-county studies. For the areas bordering Herefordshire, these included glossaries for Radnorshire (1881), Shropshire (1879), south Worcestershire (1875), west Worcestershire (1882), south-east Worcestershire (1893) and Gloucestershire (1890). Nationally, Victorian efforts would eventually culminate in Joseph Wright's monumental six-volume *The English Dialect Dictionary*, published between 1898 and 1905, and containing some 80,000 entries.

Francis Tebbs Havergal (1829–90)

Clergymen were particularly well-placed to compile lists of dialect words. They were typically well-educated, and with some means and leisure time at their disposal. Crucially, they were also in day-to-day contact with their flock – the uneducated, working-class men and women whom Lewis and others identified as the principal speakers of dialect. One such clergyman was Francis Tebbs Havergal, whose *Herefordshire Words & Phrases, Colloquial and Archaic* was published in 1887. He was well supported in his venture by others of the cloth: of the 179 subscribers listed in the front of his book, 77 were fellow clergymen.

Havergal was vicar of Upton Bishop at the time, and wrote several books, including on Hereford Cathedral. The driving impulse for his glossary (compiled almost half a century after Lewis's and containing 1,300 entries) was a recognition of a process that continues to this day – namely that of language loss (what modern dialectologists call 'lexical attrition'):

> Curious words and phrases may be heard at our Infirmaries, County Courts, Savings Banks, Markets, Railway Stations, and Auctions; and at other places where rustics congregate. But in all these places a great change has been coming on; old customs are dying out, and many old words are becoming obsolete.

Dr Henry Graves Bull (1818–85)

Other Herefordshire writers, while not primarily concerned with dialect, also compiled and published word-lists. One such was Dr Henry Graves Bull, founder and early president of the Woolhope Naturalists' Field Club, and editor of its *Transactions*. Better known for his work on the glorious *Herefordshire Pomona* (1876–85), his *Notes on the Birds of Herefordshire* was published in 1888. This contains an appendix of local bird names for the county, including *Bottle Tit*,

Canbottle, *Mumruffin* and *Ragamuffin* for the long-tailed tit, and *Hickle*, *Rain-bird*, *Stock-heckle*, *Storm-bird*, *Yaffil* and *Yuckle* for the green woodpecker (see p. 175).

Winifred Leeds (1883–1984)

In 1959, midway through the following century, the Woolhope Club elected its first female president, Winifred Leeds (one of the first three women admitted to the club in 1954). With a background in languages, Leeds became an expert in dialect use in Herefordshire, and published *Herefordshire Speech* (*the south-west Midland dialect as spoken in Herefordshire and its environs*) in 1974. Like Havergal and Ella Mary Leather (*The Folk-Lore of Herefordshire*, 1912) before her, Leeds was fascinated by customs and folklore. As well as scholarly analysis of the dialect and its historical sources – and the glossary itself, with around 2,000 entries – her book includes euphemisms, gibes, 'picturesque and pithy phrases', and a chapter on weather rhymes and proverbs. Entries in the latter range from the enigmatic: 'Till St. James' Day be come and gone, / There may be hops and there may be none'; to the poetic: 'Moon on its back, holds water in its lap'.

Andrew Haggard (1892–1976)

By coincidence, *Herefordshire Speech* was one of two dialect glossaries for Herefordshire published in the early 1970s. While Winifred Leeds was busy in Ross-on-Wye, in nearby Ledbury, Andrew Haggard was compiling his *Dialect and Local Usages of Herefordshire*, published in 1972. As Haggard makes clear (and in contrast to Leeds), his collection 'makes no pretence to scholarship'. Settling in Ledbury after the First World War as a fruit-grower 'always in close association with working men', Haggard learned local words and phrases first-hand and partly out of necessity. For 50 years he jotted them down, and personally heard most of his listed words in use. Together, he and Leeds confirm the richness and endurance of traditional dialect use in Herefordshire well into the second half of the twentieth century.

Sources

So, what of the following glossary and the words it contains? There are two broad headings under which one might consider this question: the *sources* of the words, and the *subjects* of the words – how the words came to be, and what they have to say.

While the glossary includes some information on sources, it does not include a detailed etymology for every word listed. Some general observations on linguistic sources, however, may usefully be added here. Firstly, Germanic dialects, Old Norse and Norman French in particular – introduced through raids and invasion, migration and settlement in the early medieval period (*c.*400–1100) – represent the wellsprings from which not only modern English took shape, but also regional variation and dialect. These sources are reflected in the glossary in words, for example, of Germanic ancestry (including *frum*, *gore*, *nisgal*, *peasen* and *vern*); and Old Norse in the case of words such as *spadger* or *spadjuck* (house sparrow). The lineage of these latter words can be traced through the northern dialect word *spag*, and the Scots *spurg*, to the Old Norse *sporr* (sparrow).

Following the Norman Conquest in the eleventh century, French began to exert an influence, and the glossary contains a significant number of words of Norman and Old French ancestry (including *boodget*, *cooch*, *dishabils*, *gout*, *langet*, *shespy* and *tissock*). That French should be discernible in the traditional dialect words of Herefordshire is not surprising, given the intensity of Norman activity and influence in this region after 1066. William I, deeming the conquest of Wales both unnecessary and too costly in terms of resources and manpower, chose instead to install trusted countrymen in the key settlements of Chester, Shrewsbury and Hereford, in order to defend the border. Over the next 200 years, the Welsh Marches expanded to become a dynamic and turbulent buffer zone made up of nearly 50 semi-autonomous lordships, many administered by powerful families of Norman lineage.

It might be expected, given the proximity too of native Welsh speakers, that the Welsh language would also be reflected throughout the glossary. This is the case, but only to an extent. While there are words of Welsh origin – for example *butty*, *flannen*, *gwarrell*, *keffel*, *prill*, *ross*, *timsarah* and *tump* – it is perhaps surprising there are not more of them. After all, the border here shifted back and forth, and large numbers of Welsh speakers lived and were heard in Herefordshire (such that this was once known as 'Herefordshire in Wales'). So why are there not more words of Welsh origin? Cultural entrenchment or resistance to influence arising from historical suspicion and enmity are both possibilities. It could also be, however, that the challenges of Welsh pronunciation to some extent limited the English uptake of Welsh words.

Besides the various linguistic sources discussed above, the influence of popular literature can also be traced throughout the glossary. The most notable of these sources are the works of Chaucer, writing in the first half of the fourteenth century (from which *brat*, *hege sugge*, *mullock*, *nesh* and *stare* are examples); and Shakespeare, writing in the decades to either side of 1600 (from which *afeard*, *eaning*, *giglot*, *kecksies* and *malkin* are examples).

Subjects

In terms of subject matter, and what the words have to say, the glossary also reveals much. In the preface to his 1839 glossary (see above), George Cornewall Lewis observed, 'A pastoral and agricultural region will preserve more of the terms which belong to husbandry: more of the ancient terms of art will be preserved in a manufacturing district.' This is strikingly the case in the following glossary, with more than 600 words (around 20% of the total) relating directly to farming.

That so many farming terms appear in a list of words now lost from everyday use says much about the changes witnessed in agriculture. Up to the Second World War, farming was dominated by horse-power and manpower; the agricultural landscape by a patchwork of small fields and farmsteads. After the war, increased mechanisation saw tractors replace horses and fewer men employed on the land. Many farms were consolidated and fields enlarged, with the loss of around half of hedgerows in the second half of the twentieth century. As farming evolved, so too the language of farming, in order to verbalise particular activities and implements. And as older methods and tools became outmoded, so too the words used to describe them.

Take for example two simple farm implements: the flail and the scythe. The evolution of each brought with it a wealth of accompanying words. In Herefordshire, the flail was also known as a *threshel*, *thresher*, *drashel* or *dreshel*. The part held by the worker was the *handstaff* (made of willow). The upper (striking) part was the *swingel*, *pelt*, *nile* or *ile* (made of holly). U-shaped pieces of ash called *caplings* were lashed to the ends of each, and the two parts linked with a *capling string* or *thonk* (made of raw-hide or twisted eel skin). The latter word (from 'thong' rather than the sound made when in use) led to the flail also being called *two-sticks-and-a-thonk*.

The scythe too has a rich vocabulary all of its own, including the following names for its various parts: *sned*, *pole ring*, *tang*, *lower ring*, *grass-nail*, *quinel*, *clet*, *nib*, *tut*, *vantage nib* and *cayther*. According to Andrew Haggard, sharpening was done first with a round sharpening stone called a *rubber*, and then with 'a tapering square-sectioned piece of ivy-wood kept smeared with a mixture of lard and brick-dust' called a *ripe*. If the blade had a dull edge, it would ring when sharpened with the rubber; if sharp the stone would 'hiss' along the blade, and if really sharp it would 'whisper'.

The loss of horses from farms after the Second World War saw a corresponding loss of words. For the rural soundscape, none may have been more noticeable than those used by waggoners. The clop of hooves, the rattle and crunch of wheels, the creak of *thripples* – these sounds were accompanied by the calls of the waggoner to his horses. For different parts of

Herefordshire, different calls could be heard. In the east of the county, the command to 'turn right' was *gee-back!*, in the north-east it was *aet!*, and in the north-west it was *zick!* But *hoot!*, *see back!* and *t'right!* were also used for the same instruction (see Waggoners' calls, p. 178).

Herefordshire is cider and hop country, and both are well represented in the glossary. For cider, there is an array of words for the paraphernalia used both to make and to store cider: *chase*, *cheese*, *cooler*, *costrel*, *devil*, *dripping bags*, *gaun*, *hairs*, *piggin*, *scratter*, *trin* and *tundish*. Also for the quality and flavour of cider: *belly vengeance*, *churt*, *hoshy*, *pricked*, *squeal-pig* and *swillick*.

For hops, the language is dominated by the cycle of activities, from preparing the *hopyard* to processing the picked hops. Hopyards were *wired* using a *monkey*; hops were picked into *cribs*; the volume of picked hops gauged using a *bushel basket* and recorded by a *tally-man* using a *tally-stick*. Hops were dried in a *hop kiln*, then shovelled with a *skippet* into a *hop-pocket*, and compacted with a *hop-bagger*. The full pocket was *prawled* shut, leaving two ears at the top known as *cods*.

Hop-picker is the term given not only to the farm labourer (typically seasonal) who picks the hops, but also to fine weather in late August and early September when hop-picking takes place. Specifically, to a day that starts with early mist and heavy dew, giving way to sunshine and sharp air: 'It's a real *hop-picker* today!'

The term is one of a number of weather phrases and words found in the glossary, many applicable to farming in particular. *Growing weather* is warm and wet; *falling weather* when rain or snow is expected; *open weather* when the ground is not bound by frost and is readily worked. The language of rain or changeable weather includes: *cruddley* or *cruddledy* for a mackerel sky; *glemmy* (north Herefordshire) and *puthery* (south Herefordshire) for close, thundery weather; *clibberty* for sticky; *ketchy* or *caz'ulty* for unsettled or changeable; *gnats flying over* for a slight drizzle; *ambling* or *pecking* for starting to rain or spotting with rain; *dabbley* or *dabbledly* for showery; *full flush* or *empt* for pouring with rain; *waggoner's rain* for torrential rain falling 'straight down or straight across'; and *thunder berries* for great drops of rain. *Crooly* for cold and wet; *dawny* for damp and dank; *frem* for fresh and chilly. *Whiffeldy* for a light and variable wind. *Comesnow* is the imminence of snow, and when snow falls *the old woman is feathering her goose.*

Weather lore can also be found in words for flora and fauna. In Herefordshire, a name given to the scarlet pimpernel is the *poor man's weather glass*, as the flowers open only when the sun shines. (In Somerset, the scarlet pimpernel is called the *change of the weather*, *grandfather's weatherglass* or *old man's weatherglass*; in Wiltshire it is the *ploughman's weatherglass*, and in several other counties it is the *shepherd's weatherglass*).

More than 350 words in the glossary relate to plants or animals, their number and richness suggesting a far closer rapport with the natural world than is general today. Nationally, some of the richest local language relates to plants. Geoffrey Grigson's 1955 book, *The Englishman's Flora* contains 5,500 local names for plants, including for example more than 100 names for the common and widespread Herb Robert – one of which used in Herefordshire is *thunder and lightning.*

Predictably, many plants are named for their appearance: *butter and eggs* or *eggs and bacon* (yellow toadflax), *doddering dillies* (quaking grass), *May blobs* (marsh marigold), *peal-of-bells* (campanula), *shoes and stockings* (birdsfoot trefoil) and *snotty-berry* (yew). *Bloody fingers* are foxgloves, but so are *fairy gloves* and *snawps*. Others are named for their taste: *bread and cheese* (hawthorn) and *sour sally* (sorrel); or for their effect when taken, including as folk-medicine: *black doctor* (water figwort), *crazies* (buttercups) and *piss-a-bed* (dandelion, from the French *pissenlit* – literally 'piss in bed', on account of its diuretic properties). A *tisty-tosty* is a nosegay of cowslips (first recorded in 1568, from the Middle English *tyte tust*). *Kiss-me-at-the-garden-gate* is woodruff. Its sweet-scented dried leaves were used to stuff mattresses, and single leaf whorls were even kept in pocket watches in the eighteenth century, for a waft of fragrance when the watch-case was opened. *Granny's bonnets* are columbine flowers; *granny's gown* is fumitory and *granny's pincushions*, scabious.

Birds too are named for their appearance: *firebrand tail* (redstart) and *seven-coloured linnet* (goldfinch); others for their habits and habitats: *bud bird* (bullfinch) and *nettle-creeper* (whitethroat). Bird calls are vividly conjured up by *devil screecher* or *jack squealer* (swift), *pink* or *twink* (chaffinch) and the tremulous *jelly hooter* (owl). As with some plants, certain birds were thought to be harbingers of weather. The mistle thrush, which was said to sing with greater gusto during stormy weather, is the *storm cock* or *storm screech*; the green woodpecker, the *storm-bird* or *rain-bird*, and the chaffinch, the *wet-bird*. A *wizzel* is a dipper, so-named for its 'zit, zit' call or its whirring flight (or perhaps both). *Scribbling schoolmaster* and *writing lark* are names for the yellowhammer, after the ink-like scribbles on its eggs; and *blue Isaac* for the blue-egged dunnock or hedge sparrow (names that would have made sense to many more people, including children, before egg-collecting was outlawed in 1954). *Bottle tit* and *canbottle* are names for the long-tailed tit, whose distinctive nest is bottle-shaped.

For wild mammals the glossary has: *archenstraw* or *artist-raw* (mouse or shrew); *cat*, *puss* or *Sarah* (hare); *fitchet* (polecat, stoat or ferret); *fluttermouse* (bat); *hedgepig* or *urchin* (hedge-hog); *maister teddy* (badger); *clover-snapper* or *scunny* (rabbit); and *hoont* or *oont* (mole). The latter yields *oontitump* for a molehill, and by the same logic an *anty tump* is an anthill.

Aside from the unfamiliar words, the glossary also contains a large number of corruptions and non-standard spellings of familiar words. For the letter A, for example, there are more than 20 such words, including *abundation* (abundance), *ackern* (acorn), *ahthern* (hawthorn), *allus* (always), *angkercher* (handkerchief), *apricock* (apricot, used by Shakespeare), *archat* (orchard) and *atomy* (skeleton, from 'anatomy'). These represent local variants or derivations of standard words. What is less easy to decipher is which represent locally accepted spellings and which phonetic transcriptions from the spoken word of the dialect speaker, as deduced by the interviewer for the purposes of recording the word. Either way, such words provide life-affirming testimony of the local resistance of English speakers to the standardisation of the language – and this well into the twentieth century, almost 500 years after efforts to such an end were first begun.

THE GLOSSARY

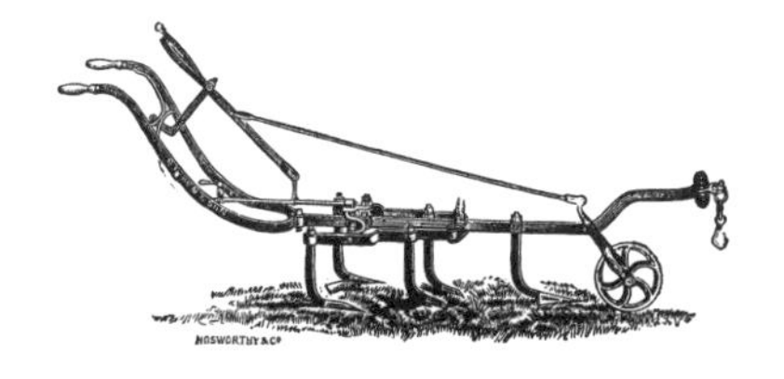

ABBREVIATIONS USED IN THE GLOSSARY

PARTS OF SPEECH

adj.	adjective
adv.	adverb
conj.	conjunction
n.	noun
prep.	preposition
pron.	pronoun
v.	verb

WRITERS

AH	Andrew Haggard
FTH	Francis Tebbs Havergal
GCL	George Cornewall Lewis
WL	Winifred Leeds

NB *bracketed place-names occur intermittently throughout the glossary. These represent specific settlements or localities in which the word was recorded in use; however, the word's use was not necessarily restricted to that place*

A

abear *v.* (also **abide**) endure, tolerate

able *adj.* well-to-do, rich; capable in money matters. 'He did better out of the deal, being an *able* man'

aboove *prep.* above

aboove-a-bit *adv.* very much, greatly. 'I like it *aboove-a-bit*'

abundation *n.* abundance

abuseful *adj.* abusive, rude

accord *v.* (pronounced 'accard') agree. 'I *accord* with you'

ackern *n.* (also **ackum, atchorn, atchurn**) acorn. Once used in the common proverb 'as sound as an *ackern*'

acquaintance *n.* sweetheart. 'He's her *acquaintance* now'

acre wide *n.* a piece of land 220 yards (10 chains) long and 22 yards (1 chain) wide. The expression probably derives from the fact that, in general, the length of a furrow in common fields was 220 yards or 1 furlong (furrow-long), so that a stretch 22 yards wide would equal 1 acre

adland *n.* (also **addland, addlum, adlant**) headland: the strip of land at the end of a furrow for the plough to turn

adle *adj.* (also **addle, aydle**) rotten (especially of eggs)

aet! go to the right. See Waggoners' calls, p. 178

afeard *adj.* afraid, fearful (Shakespearean)

aftermath *n.* the year's second crop of hay

against *prep.* (also **agin**) by, or by the time that. 'He'll get here *against* lunchtime'

ahthern *n.* hawthorn

aidled *adj.* addled, discombobulated

ainer *v.* have not. 'I *ainer* seen him recently'

airyated *adj.* 1. aerated; 2. het up, agitated

aizack *n.* hedge sparrow, dunnock

all-about *adj.* light-headed, delirious; confused, muddled

all-hell-and-no-notion phrase used to describe a person working hard but ineffectively and with little skill

all in his clothes in his vestments (of a clergyman etc.)

all-so *conj.* (also **also**) except, all but, save (as in 'all save'). 'He ate all the apples *all-so* this one'

alley-bo *n.* wheelbarrow

allus *adv.* (also **ollus**) always

ambligator *n.* (also **amblingator, ambling gaiter**) long-armed pruner or clippers, for pruning out-of-reach branches (LEDBURY). In J.C. Louden's *Dictionary of Gardening* (1827) the implement is called an 'averruncator'. *Amblingator* (COLWALL)

ambling *v., adj.* said of rain that has just begun to fall. 'The rain was *ambling* as we got home' (MON BORDER)

ammer *n.* yellowhammer (from the German for 'bunting')

aneaoust *prep.* (also **neaous**) near to. 'He lives *aneaoust* me'

anent *prep.* (also **anenst, anunt, anunst**) 1. against, opposite; 2. close to, next to

angkercher *n.* handkerchief

angleberries *n.* warts, particularly on cattle

anighst *prep.* near. 'I wouldn't go *anighst* her'

anna *v.* am not. 'I *anna* happy with him'

ant *n.* (also **anty**) aunt; auntie

anty tump *n.* anthill

apern *n.* (also **aspern**) apron

apple-headed *adj.* of a woodland tree whose branches are growing lower on the trunk than is usual (MON BORDER)

apricock *n.* apricot (used by Shakespeare e.g. in *Richard II*)

ar dun! (also **a done!**) stop it! have done! (e.g. to a child)

ara *pron.*, *adv.* any, ever. 'Have you *ara* hay to bring in?'

arc *n.* 'a peculiar cloud or cirrus across the sky, N. to S., seen in the morning and evening only on rare occasions ... said to be "pointed, bright at the ends and very pretty." I have found this word only in a low damp part of Upton Bishop among very old people' (FTH). 'A mare's tail cloud, or cirrus, in the form of a streak across the sky' (GCL)

archat *n.* (also **archut, archert**) orchard

archenstraw *n.* (also **ardistraw, ardy straw, artistraw, ardistril, hardistraw**) a shrew or mouse; a field mouse or harvest mouse (*hardistraw* is recorded in KENTCHURCH)

arg *v.* to argue, to wrangle. 'I wouldn't *arg* with him'

argufy *v.* signify, matter. 'It doesn't *argufy* what he says'

argy *n.* (pronounced with a hard 'g') a hurdle slung across water to stop cattle wandering up and down a stream (from the Welsh *ar gwy* = on Wye) (EWYAS HAROLD)

arkard *adj.* (also **okkerd**) awkward. 'He's an *arkard* old sod'

arl *n.* (also **aul, orl, orle**) alder tree

arl leasow *n.* alder plantation

arn cag *n.* (also **horn cag**) 'As tough as an old *arn cag*': i.e. hard and unyielding (*cag* probably from 'keg')

arrand *n.* errand

article *n.* contemptuous or abusive term often preceded by 'old': 'You dirty old *article*!'

as *pron.* that. 'He isn't the same man *as* I saw yesterday'

as you've a mind as you wish, as you please

asgall *n.* (also **askal, askel, asker**) newt

ashen *adj.* made of ash

ashett *n.* a plate (possibly from the French *assiette*)

ashore *adj.* ajar, as of a door. 'Leave the door *ashore*'

asiden *prep.* on one side. 'I've left your glasses *asiden*'

asp *n.* aspen tree

asplining *v.* prancing about. 'Stop *asplining* and sit down'

assgut *n.* (also **ascot**) of sheep, when the gut is inverted through the rectum, this is known as having the '*assgut* out' (literally 'arse-gut')

atchurn *v.* to gather acorns. 'He's *atchurning* in the woods'

ater *prep.* after

atomy *n.* a skeleton (a corruption of 'anatomy')

attack *v.* undertake. 'I will *attack* the journey tomorrow'

audacious *adj.* rude, insolent

aulen *adj.* adjectival form of *aul* or *arl*: 'an *aulen* coppice'

avoirdupoised *adj.* in doubt about doing a thing. 'I'm all *avoirdupoised*' (EARDISLAND). The word derives from the old French *aveir de peis*, meaning 'goods of weight' and refers to an international system of weight measurement dating from the thirteenth century, primarily used by merchants for the purposes of trade. Its appropriation as a term of befuddlement may derive from the bewildering variations to the weight system as used by different nations at different points in history

away *v.* bear, endure. 'I can't *away* it' (GOLDEN VALLEY)

away-ta-go! off you go! (N HEREFS)

away to go now we can get going (e.g. after being held up)

awhile *v.* to spare time to do something. 'I'm busy and can't *awhile* to meet with him' (EARDISLAND)

axe *v.* (also **ax, aks**) to ask

aya! to the near side; come over (to a team of horses). See Waggoners' calls, p. 178

ayriff *n.* (also **herriff**) cleavers, goose grass

B

baa! baa! (also **baa-ho!**) call to sheep. See Calls to animals, p. 177

babby *n.* baby

baby's bottle *n.* Jack-in-the-pulpit (plant) (GOLDEN VALLEY)

back-assed *adj.* things done the wrong way around. 'His way of doing things is all *back-assed*' (PEMBRIDGE)

back-friend *n.* a torn cuticle

back-side *n.* a back garden or back yard

back-sided *adj.* of a house, facing away from sun (BRAMPTON BRYAN)

backarder *adv.* further backwards

backen *v.* 1. to stunt, to keep back (particularly of crops). 'The cold weather *backened* growth of the wheat'; 2. to decrease, to lessen (especially of pain)

backer *adv., n.* (also **backy**) 1. further back; 2. tobacco

backwards and forwards, not a word further there's an end to the matter (HEREFORD)

badge *v.* to cut, especially thistles, weeds etc. (from *bodge* or *botch*, thus a job that needs no skill) (MON BORDER)

badger *n.* a dealer in poultry, fruit etc.

badging-hook *n.* (also **bagging-hook**) hooked blade for trimming hedges or cutting down thistles etc.; broader than a sickle and not serrated

baff *v.* (also **buff**) to stammer. 'He was *baffing* and we couldn't make out a word he said' (STAUNTON-ON-WYE)

bag *n., v.* 1. cow's udder; 2. to cut peas with a *badging-hook*

bailey *n.* 1. a seed-barrow for planting clover or grass seeds (E HEREFS); 2. an area of land under a bailiff

bait *n.* a snack or light meal, generally taken in the morning; elevenses

bald-rib *n.* spare rib

ballywray *v.* (also **ballyrag**) to abuse, to scold coarsely. 'I bet she *ballywrayed* you proper'

band-hay *n.* inferior quality hay

bandy *n.* an old game played with bent sticks (hence *bandy* legs, i.e. bowed legs)

bang *v.* (also **bank**) to knock apples from a tree

banger *n.* (also **slammer, slamming post**) the post against which a gate shuts

banky piece *n.* a field on a steep slope

bannut *n.* walnut, walnut tree (cut timber is still 'walnut')

banter *v.* to bargain

barberris *adj.* cruel, pitiless; barbarous (EARDISLAND)

bargain *n.* task (a hard *bargain* = a difficult task) (LINGEN)
barm *n.*, *v.* 1. yeast; 2. to leaven for bread-making
barth *n.* a sow spayed when young
bash *n.* 1. the mass of the roots of a tree; 2. the front of a bull's or a pig's head; 3. a deranged person; 4. the palm of the hand. See *batch*
baste *v.* to thrash or flog
basting *n.* a thrashing or flogging
bat *n.* 1. a wooden tool used for breaking up clods of earth (N HEREFS); 2. great speed. 'He was going at a terrific *bat*'
batch *n.* (also **bap**) 1. the palm of the hand; 2. a *batch* or *batch* cake is a small flat loaf (ROSS)
bath *n.* female pig, sow. 'The *bath's* had her piglets'
bathering *v.*, *adj.* 1. roozling or ruffling in the dust (particularly said of partridges); 2. shaking or knocking down fruit (apples etc.) (LEDBURY)
batterkin *n.* when horses are working abreast, each horse's traces are attached to a *batterkin* (a piece of iron forming part of the harness, which keeps the horses spaced). This in turn is attached to the *land-tree* (*whipple-tree*)
batterpins *n.* draught trees, grown as wind-breaks
baulk *n.*, *v.* 1. a ridge; 2. to *baulk the wind* = to erect shelters against the wind (e.g. in a *hopyard*)
bayly *n.* bailiff
bean for a pea phrase used to denote a lack of generosity. 'He wouldn't give you a *bean for a pea*'
bearbine *n.* (also **bell-bine**) (*bear* pronounced 'beer') bindweed, *convolvulus* (plant)
beast-house *n.* cowhouse (WIGMORE)

beaumonteg *n.* any sort of useful preparation or mixture, from rat-poison to homemade fillers for patch repairs. 'Fetch me down some *beaumonteg*'. *Webster's International Dictionary* of 1924 defines *beaumantage* as a cement used for making joints etc. In a report about the Tay Bridge disaster of 1879, *beaumontegg* is referred to as a mixture of beeswax, lamp-black, rosin and iron turnings used to conceal flaws in the bridge's defective metalwork

becall *v.* to abuse violently. 'She flew into a rage and *becalled* him something terrible'

bed *n.* the floor of a waggon or cart

bee-bole *n.* an alcove in a wall for keeping bee *skeps*

beechen *adj.* made of beech

beestings *n.* the first milk after calving

beethy *adj.* (also **beethered, beevy, beezy**) 1. shrivelled, shrunken, withered but not desiccated, wilted (crops etc.); 2. soft, over-ripe (particularly apples and pears); 3. wet, limp, cold (applied to hay and hops that have not dried properly) (BRAMPTON BRYAN); 4. underdone (applied to cooked meat). *Beevy* and *beezy* (GOLDEN VALLEY)

beetle *n.* (also **bittle**) a wooden mallet for knocking in hedge stakes or driving wedges into wood. A *ring-beetle* has iron bands around the hammer. A *bot-beetle* is used for breaking up clods of hard earth. *Bittle* (MON BORDER)

before-handed *conj.* in advance (MON BORDER)

begrudged *adj.* unduly weak or weakened. Tea *begrudged* = very weak tea

bell-ail *n.* (also **bell-oil**) a thrashing (WHITCHURCH)

bell-bine *n.* bindweed (plant) (GOLDEN VALLEY)

bellock *v.* 1. to bellow (cattle); 2. to cry loudly (children)

bellocking *n., adj.* (also **bullocking**) 1. the lowing of cattle; 2. noisy, rude

bellrag *v.* to scold in a clamorous manner

belly vengeance *n.* cider that is so acidic it is undrinkable

belly wambles *n.* an uncomfortable sensation in the bowels; the gripes. 'That cider's given me the *belly wambles*'

benefit *n.* trouble, bother. 'It caused me much *benefit*'

b'ent *v.* (also **beyunt**) am not, are not. 'I *b'ent* coming over'

bent two double *adj.* greatly bent over, obviously stooping

bents *n.* withered stalks of grass; seed-stalks of grass

besom *n.* 1. a shrew (an insult applied to a woman); 2. (also **beesom, bizzom**) a twig broom (typically of birch) for sweeping leaves etc.

bespoke *adj.* marked for death (ARCHENFIELD)

bessy-boy *n.* odd-job boy (BRAMPTON BRYAN)

bessy-coddle *n.* (also **bessy**) said of a man who interferes with a woman's business

bett *adj., v.* 1. beaten; 2. to pare or cut turf

better nor more than, better than. 'You're *better nor* that'

betwattled *adj.* confused, distressed, moithered. 'His riddling left me quite *betwattled*' (LEOMINSTER)

bewray *v.* to defile with excrement

beyond *v.* to get the better of. 'I can't get *beyond* him'

bib *n.* a small projection or bump

bible-backed *adj.* used to describe rounded parts that should be angular, specifically of bricks that have been distorted and deformed by over-firing

bidding *n.* an invitation to a wedding or a funeral

biddy *n.* a sitting hen

biff *n.* beef

big-sorted *adj.* (also **bigsorted**) proud, of one who puts on airs. 'He's a *big-sorted* so-and-so' (N HEREFS)

billy-ploughboy *n.* a 'water' (or grey) wagtail (WIGMORE)

billy ruffin *n.* (also **mum ruffin**) long-tailed tit

bine *n.* a twining stalk (e.g. a hop *bine*)

bing *n.* a passage in a cowhouse, extending along the heads of the stalls (WIGMORE)

binna *v.* a negative form of 'to be': it's not been

birdie! birdie! call to guinea fowl. See Calls to animals, p. 177

bird's eye *n.* germander speedwell (plant)

bishop *n.* an overly large tump of manure

bishopped *adj.*, *v.* confirmed (in the religious sense)

bist? (also **bista?**) you are, are you? '*Bista* coming down?'

bit of bad luck an unmarried woman becoming pregnant was commonly described as having had a *bit of bad luck*

bite-in-hand *n.* a hunk of cheese and bread; a snack to take away, for lunch at work etc. (BRAMPTON BRYAN)

black doctor *n.* water figwort (plant) (GOLDEN VALLEY)

black-pole *n.* a long piece of unwrought timber, about as much as a man can carry. Poles left standing in a copse are sometimes referred to as *black-poles*

black stare *n.* (also **steer**) starling

blackie *n.* blackbird (ROSS)

blackthorn winter *n.* a winter that turns very cold late in the season (i.e. at the time the blackthorn blossoms)

blast *n.* an inflammation of some external part of the body

bleggin *v.* cutting down thistles etc.; tidying up ditches. 'He's in the top field *bleggin* nettles' (N HEREFS)

blight *n.*, *v.* 1. 'the climatic condition when the horizon (alone) is dark and hazy and has the appearance of being obscured by a dark cloud' (AH); 2. 'He shook his *blight* at me' = he was cocky or impertinent towards me

blind *adj.* plants that fail to flower are said to be *blind*; also, blossom which does not come to fruit

blizzey *n.* (also **blizzy**) a bonfire (FOWNHOPE)

blob *n.* a blister

blocks *n.* logs cut for burning indoors

bloody butcher *n.* wild hyacinth (N HEREFS)

bloody fingers *n.* foxgloves. 'Dead man's fingers' appears e.g. in Shakespeare's *Hamlet* (iv. 7.)

blouse *n.* 1. pollen of grass; 2. the mites found in old cider

blow *n.*, *v.* (pronouced as in 'now') 1. blossom; 2. to blossom. 'The trees are in *blow*'; 'The trees are starting to *blow*'

blub *n.*, *adj.* a swelling, swollen. 'His face was *blubbed* up'

blue butcher *n.* early purple orchid; also iris

blue hawk *n.* sparrow hawk

blue Isaac *n.* hedge sparrow or dunnock. *Blue* from the colour of its eggs; *Isaac* from Old English *hege sugge* = 'hedge-sucker' (WL)

blue-tail *n.* fieldfare (bird)

blunder out *v.* to puzzle it out

blunderbush *n.* a stumbler, someone unsteady on their feet (N HEREFS)

blutter *v.*, *n.* (also **blutter and hack**) stutter, stammer

bock *n.*, *adv.*, *v.* back

bodge *n., v.* (also **boodge, botch, buge**) 1. to fill up holes in a hedge with trimmings (*browse*); 2. a knock or blow; to knock; 3. a prick or puncture with a pin or needle; 4. a temporary or poor quality repair

bodger *n.* a tool or implement for knocking in hedge stakes (W HEREFS); 2. an inexpert workman (N HEREFS)

body *n.* a term of commiseration, denoting deficiency. 'He's a poor, simple *body*'

body-horse *n.* the second horse in a team of four

bogie *n.* (also **bugabo**) a ghost

bolting *n.* (pronounced 'bawten' or 'bowtin') a bundle or sheaf of straw (sometimes specifically of long straw, generally of 14lbs and tied with two bands)

bomboly *adj.* (also **bomely**) awkward to fit. In walling, a *bomboly* stone is one that is hard to find a place for

bonds *n.* twigs for tying up bundles of faggots

boo *n.* (pronounced 'bow') a bug or louse

boodget *n.* (also **booget**) a container or bucket (from the French *bougette* = a pouch)

book *n.* the *book* = the Bible

book-craft *n.* (also **book learning**) literary pursuits, reading

boon *n.* (also **bun**) a rope of straw used for tying up a bottle

boosey *n.* (also **boosy, boosin**) 1. a cowhouse; 2. a manger or the feeding passage behind the mangers in a cowhouse

boosey pasture *n.* 1. a field next to a cowhouse; 2. pasture retained until May by a tenant quitting his farm at Candlemass (2 February), this being a right for tenants under these circumstances (GOLDEN VALLEY)

borrow *v.* to seek shelter (from the wind)

boss *n.*, *v.* 1. a head of clover; 2. to cut off clover heads so the second-grown heads can yield seed (*bossing* clover)

bosser *n.* a machine used to extract clover seed

bost *v.* to burst open

bot *v.* to beat (ASHPERTON)

bot-beetle *n.* a wooden mallet used for breaking up clods of hard earth

botcher *n.* a salmon of between 4lb and 7lb (a term more common on the Severn than on the Wye)

bottle *n.* 1. a small wooden barrel or keg with a carrying handle, in which a workman carried his cider, usually holding 4–6 pints; 2. a heap of straw or hay; 3. 'He's no *bottle*' = he's no good

bottle tit *n.* a long-tailed tit (for the shape of its nest)

bottom *n.* 1. 'The *bottom* and both ends of it' = the whole story (S HEREFS); 2. 'To stand on a firm *bottom*' = to be trustworthy (W HEREFS); 3. 'To have no *bottom*' = to be untrustworthy or unreliable

boughten *adj.* bought. Used mainly to distinguish shop-bought goods from home-made. 'That's *boughten* butter'

bounce out *v.* to sulk, to go off in a huff

bouncing Bet *n.* (also **bouncing Bessie**) soapwort (plant)

boundacious adj. profuse, abundant

bountiful *adj.* fat and well. 'I'm stuffed and *bountiful*'

bout *n.* two consecutive *strokes* of the plough or other implement, out and back again

bouter *n.* (also **boater, bowter**) a plough with two mould-boards used for '*bouting* out' ground (forming ridges) for planting potatoes

bowk *n.* nave or stock (hub) of a wooden cart wheel

bowket *n.* bouquet

bowler *n.* boulder

box *v.*, *n.* 1. of a horse: to use teeth and hooves aggressively when approached or handled; 2. the treasury of a club. 'On the *box*' = drawing an allowance from club funds

boychap *n.* a lad

brabble *n.*, *v.* a quarrel; to quarrel

bracking *v.* the chipping or cracking of eggshells when hatching starts (N HEREFS)

brageant *adj.* bombastic, pompous, long-winded

braggable *adj.* worth boasting about

brand tail *n.* (also **brant-tail, brantail, branter, fire-brand tail, kitty brantail**) redstart (bird)

branners *adj.* first class, top grade. 'My spuds are absolute *branners*'

brash *n.* beds of loose, softish stone, such as are often encountered locally when ploughing

brashy *adj.* said of the readily-worked soil of e.g. a river terrace that contains small pebbles etc. (WHITCHURCH)

brat *n.*, *v.* 1. a dark-coloured overall; 2. to cover with soil. Charcoal-burners *brat* their stacked wood (MON BORDER)

brawn *n.* boar (W HEREFS)

bread and cheese *n.* hawthorn. So-called because the young leaves in particular are edible, with a nutty flavour

bree *n.* (also **breese**) the warble-fly, a cattle parasite (N HEREFS)

bren it! burn it! (an exclamation)

brenth *n.* breadth

brevet *v.* (also **brevett, brevit, brivet, bruvet, bruvit**) 1. to behave unquietly, to fuss about; to be fidgety or restless; 2. to fossick or search out; to rummage or pry

breveting *v.* gadding about. 'The new lambs are *breveting* in the orchard'

brightsmith *n.* a tinsmith (S HEREFS)

brim *n.* a boar

brimming *adj.* on heat. 'The mare is *brimming*'

brittle *v.* to examine closely, to scrutinise

brittling *adj.* agitating for a clear out, spring clean etc.

broccolo *n.* broccoli

brock *n.* badger (widespread)

brontitis *n.* (also **brownkites, browntitus**) bronchitis

brot *n.* loose straw (KENTCHURCH)

browse *n., v.* (also **browce, brouse, broust, trouse**) 1. brushwood or hedge trimmings; to cut brushwood (S HEREFS). In the fourteenth century, the word was used for small branches and twigs, particularly of holly cut by foresters for deer to feed on; 2. the small bits of wood left over after cordwood and faggots have been cut from a felled tree

browse line *n.* the height to which sheep and cattle can reach to bite from trees and vegetation

bruk *n.* (also **bruck**) a brook

brummagem *adj.* a facetious adjective deriving from 'Birmingham' and used to denote cheap or poor-quality imitations of manufactured items. 'A *brummagem* tool'

brummock *n.* a cutting hook, hedge-hook or sickle

brun *n.* a billet of wood

brush *v.* referring to hedges, to trim; referring to trees, to cut away the lower branches to admit more light

brushings *n.* small hedge-trimmings (N HEREFS)

brusling *v.* brushing roughly against. 'The cows have been kicking and *brusling* the fence'

buck *v.* to wash coarse linen by beating it with a flat wooden implement on a (*bucking*) stool placed in shallow water or by the side of a river or pool

bucking *n.* a large wash of household linen. '*Buck basket*' appears e.g. in Shakespeare's *The Merry Wives of Windsor*

buckles *n.* twigs of willow shaved flat and twisted, for securing thatch (also referred to as *buckle stuff*)

bud bird *n.* (also **budding bird**) bullfinch

budget *n.* (also **boodget**) a bucket. The word appears to have a common origin with the heraldic charge (emblem or device) of the *water-bouget*, a pair of water bags or leather bottles on a yoke, a precursor to the bucket

buff *n.*, *v.* (also **buffle**) 1. a speech impediment, stammer. 'He does *buff* a bit' (W HEREFS). A *Buffing Billy* is someone who is hard to understand; 2. to bother (SUTTON ST NICHOLAS)

bugabo *n.* a bugbear, a ghost

bugan *n.* a devil. 'To play the *bugan*' = to play the devil

bugs words *n.* boasting words

bullocking *v.*, *adj.* joking, bullying. 'Stop your *bullocking*'

bully-head *n.* tadpole (WIGMORE)

bum-baillie *n.* sheriff's officer

bumbledy *adj.* mainly of stone, meaning of awkward shape and unsuitable for building. See *bomboly*

bumbles *n.* round stones, cobbles; large water-worn stones

bumlet *n.* a round stone used for filling holes in a wall

bummer *n.* the governor, gaffer or, more loosely, proprietor

bunch *n.* a small drove of cattle. 'Get that *bunch* to market'

bunchy *adj.* rank or coarse. 'That pork's too *bunchy* to eat'

bundation *n.* (also **boundation**) an abundance, e.g. of rain, fruit etc.

bundle off *v.* (also **bundle along**) go away quickly, hurry off, scurry, scarper. '*Bundle off* you lot!'

bunt *v.* to butt with the head, as a suckling calf or lamb

burr *n.* (also **bur**) 1. the sweetbread or pancreas of an animal; 2. the elder (tree), from '*bore* tree', so-named for the way the stems are easily hollowed out by children for use as pop-guns etc.; 3. a pollard

burrough *n.* (also **burrow**) the lee or side sheltered from the wind

bursted *v.* burst. 'He *bursted* open the door'

bury *n.* (also **burry**) 1. a rabbit warren or burrow (GOLDEN VALLEY); 2. a store of roots (mangels) covered with earth

burying *n.* a funeral. 'To *fetch a burying*' = to accompany the corpse at a funeral

bush *n.* the *bush* was a globe of hawthorn which, after being singed or burnt, was brought into the farmhouse kitchen on New Years' Day, where it remained throughout the year in order to bring luck

bushel basket *n.* a basket used for measuring the amount of hops picked by a hop-picker

bussock *n.* a donkey

bustle *n.*, *v.* a bout of scolding. 'He got a sharp *bustle*'

but just only this minute, just now. 'I got here *but just*'

but middling *adj.* (also **only middling**) not at all well, very poorly. 'She's gone downhill and is *but middling*'

butt *v.* to thrust upwards. 'The carrots are *butting* well'

butter and eggs *n.* yellow toadflax (plant)

butter mit *n.* a wooden bowl used in butter-making

butty *n.* 1. a workman's mate or assistant, a close friend, as 'buddy'. Probably from the Welsh *butty* = friend; however, possibly a corruption of 'abettor' (helper); 2. one of a pair (the right shoe is the *butty* of the left) (BRAMPTON BRYAN)

buy a file *v.* to file one's petition in a bankruptcy

buzkins *n.* leggings (buskins)

by-tack *n.* (also **bytack**) literally a 'bye-take': a farm taken by a tenant who resides on another, or a piece of land held separately from and in addition to the farm, usually held for grazing; a smallholding attached to a farm (implying non-residence)

bye-blow *n.* an illegitimate child, a bastard (W HEREFS)

C

cacky *adj.* dirty, grubby, messy (probably adapted from children's usage)

caddle *n.*, *v.* 1. to bother, trouble, fuss; 2. to potter or trifle about, work at odd jobs on a farm (N HEREFS); 3. to nestle, coddle or pet; 4. to chatter

caddling *adj.* 1. foolish or silly (ASTON INGHAM); 2. false, insecure, cajoling with a view to buying anything below its value. Sometimes negatively applied to butchers: 'a *caddling* butcher'

cadger *n.* a hawker or higgler; one who goes from place to place selling in small quantities; a carrier or pedlar of small wares and goods (E HEREFS)

cadow *n.* (also **caddis**) 1. a mayfly; 2. a poor creature; a simpleton

caerlock *n.* (also **carlock, curlock**) charlock, wild mustard

caffle *n.* a ravel of silk or worsted (KENTCHURCH)

cag *n.*, *v.* 1. the stump of a tooth; 2. the broken stump of a bough; 3. to catch ones nail in something, to tear material, to rip. 'I snagged my coat and *cagged* the cloth'

cag-horse *n.* a horse kept for odd jobs (BRAMPTON BRYAN)

cag mag *n.* bad meat

canbottle *n.* (also **cannon bottle**) 1. long-tailed tit; 2. less often a skylark (WORCS BORDER, NW HEREFS)

candle of the eye *n.* the pupil of the eye

canna *v.* (also **casna**) negative of 'I can' (I cannot)

cant *v.* 1. to tell tales behind someone's back, to gossip; 2. to tip up a vessel or bottle

canting *v.* a child's expression for telling tales (PEMBRIDGE)

cantle *n.* 1. the rounded portion of a saddle; 2. a piece of bread or cheese (both Chaucer and Shakespeare use *cantle* more generally for a piece or a fragment)

capling *n.* (also **capling string**) the link in a flail

carnel *n.* (also **cornel**) corner

carpeted *v.*, *adj.* to be called in for a scolding. 'It was a silly thing he done, and he was *carpeted* for it'

carron *n.* (also **carron**) name for someone that one dislikes, a worthless fellow (a corruption of 'carrion')

cast *n.* a second swarm of bees (the third is called a *hob*)

castrel *n.* (also **costrel**) a labourer's wooden cider bottle (ASHPERTON)

cat *n.* hare (GOLDEN VALLEY)

catch out *v.* help yourself to. 'Go to the pantry and *catch out* a bottle of cider'

catching *adj.* (also **catchy**) of the weather, showery. 'It's *catching* out there so take your coat'

caterpillar *n.*, *v.* 1. cockchafer (N & W HEREFS); 2. to plague or torment

cat-lick *n.* a hurried, superficial wipe or wash

cat-lift *n.* a trapdoor (cat flap) to allow entry for the cat (MON BORDER)

cats' brains *n.* rough, clayey ground; hard to work

caults *n.* (also **coats**) colts

caup *v.* (also **cowp**) to grouse, grumble (ROSS)

cauves *n.* calves

cavings *n.* hulls of wheat

cayther *n.* (also **cradle**) an attachment to a scythe, used when cutting corn: a length of hazel or willow bent to a semi-oval shape and lashed to the *pole-ring* and again at about two feet along the *sned* at right angles to the ground. Its function was to lay the swath with the corn stalks parallel, to ease the work of the tyers who followed

caz'ulty *adj.* uncertain, as of the weather. 'It's *caz'ulty* out'

cedar *n.* a pencil (pencils used to be made of cedar wood)

chain tree *n.* laburnum (so-named because of the 'chain links' of the tumbling flowers)

char *n.* (also **cher**) a job. 'That's a cracking good *char* you done for me'

charcoal boards *n.* board sides fitted to a harvest-waggon to enable it to hold a light, bulky load such as charcoal. Before coal was in general use, farmers would send their waggons once or twice a year to the charcoal-burners in the Forest of Dean or the Wyre Forest for charcoal, mainly for hop-drying

chark *n.*, *v.*, *adj.* 1. charcoal (used for heating hop kilns); to make charcoal; 2. dry in the mouth or throat

charker *n.* a charcoal maker

charm *n.*, *v.* 1. the twittering of birds; 2. the chattering of children; 3. the sound of women's voices (MON BORDER); 4. a hum, as of bees or distant conversation. 'If you listen carefully you can hear their *charm* high on the hill'

chase *n.* a stone trough used in cider-making

chastise *v.* to question closely; to accuse

chat *v.* to gather dry sticks for kindling. The activity was used as a common excuse for children not attending school. 'He's gone *chatting*'

chats *n.* 1. small potatoes; 2. pig food; 3. small chips of wood, dry sticks, kindling wood

chatter *v.* to rebuke angrily (traditionally said of women). 'She *chattered* him for his misdemeanours'

chaw *v.*, *n.* to chew (as tobacco) (N HEREFS); 2. a pig's cheek

chawls *n.* the tines of a pike or fork

chawm *n.* a crack in the ground caused by dry weather (possibly a corruption of 'chasm')

chawnipple *n.* a bumptious or lively boy (not, as might be expected, a baby)

chear *n.* a chair

cheese *n.* 1. the *pomace* (crushed apples) in cider-making; 2. the stack of six or eight *cider-hairs* loaded with *must*, forming one pressing in cider-making; 3. thick jam made from the residue of the fruit after the juice has been extracted for jelly-making (e.g. damson cheese)

cheese-cowl *n.* a shallow tub in which cheese is made

chemist *adj.* drunk. 'He's three parts *chemist*' = he's very drunk. Related to *chemist*, drink can be *medicine* (ROSS)

cherry pie *n.* heliotrope (plant)

chevy *v.* to chase. 'To *chevy* sheep' = to chase sheep. A corruption of 'chivvy'

chi-ack *n.*, *v.* 1. a quarrel or fight; to quarrel or fight; 2. a thrashing; 3. pain. 'It gave me *chi-ack*'

chick! chick! call to hens. See Calls to animals, p. 177

chiert *adj.* (also **tiert**) 1. sore, smarting; 2. acidic, sharp (to the taste)

chig! chig! call to pigs. See Calls to animals, p. 177

childer *n.* children. '*Childer* and chicken be ollus a' pickin''

chilver *n.* a ewe lamb

chimbley *n.* (also **chimley, chimmock**) chimney

chiming *n.* of a barrel, the projecting ends (KENTCHURCH)

chin cough *n.* whooping cough (N HEREFS)

chip *n.* a small, lightweight basket used for fruit

chip out *n.* a quarrel or falling-out. 'We had a big *chip out*'

chitlins *n.* chitterlings (the small intestine of e.g. a pig)

chobble *v.* to gnaw, chew into small pieces (generally refers to rats or mice, but sometimes used e.g. for rabbits)

chobblings *n.* 1. the gnawed fragments left by rats or mice; 2. the spilt food on a child's bib

chock out *v.* to chuck out (E HEREFS)

chook! chook! call to hens. See Calls to animals, p. 177

chooky pig *n.* (also **choogy pig**) a woodlouse

chump *n.* a log of wood for burning

churchman *n.* a clergyman who was a good reader, or had a strong voice, was often referred to as 'a good *churchman*'

churm *n.* a (milk) churn

churn-owl *n.* a nightjar (bird)

churt *adj.* (also **tiert**) sharp and keen (of a person, but also of cider which has a sharp taste)

cider-hairs *n.* the woven horsehair cloths into which the *must* is placed before pressing

clam *v.* 1. to starve or kill. There is an old Herefordshire proverb 'care *clammed* the cat'; 2. to clog up

clandestical *adj.* a corruption of 'clandestine'. 'There have been *clandestical* comings and goings'

clats *n.* (also **cleats, clets**) 1. clods, hard lumps of soil; 2. the nails that hold the blade to the handle of a scythe (MONNOW VALLEY)

clave *v.* past tense of 'to cleave' (GOLDEN VALLEY)

clavvy *n.* the shelf or mantle above the grate in the kitchen (N HEREFS, BISHOPS FROME)

cleach *v.* to use a *cleaching net*

cleaching net *n.* 'a bag-net, attached to a semi-circular hoop having a transverse piece, to the centre of which a pole is fixed. The net is put gently into the stream, and drawn towards the bank when the river is in flood, and the fish draw to the sides. Called a *clinching-net* in Gloucestershire' (GCL)

clean *adj.* 1. water is said to be *clean* when it has flowed over stones; 2. land free from weeds was said to be *clean*

clean forewell clean gone away; disappeared. 'We haven't seen hide nor hair of him. He's *clean forewell*'

cleancher wipe *n.* a clean sweep

clees *n.* (also **clays, cleas**) the claws of a bird or beast. Also specifically the cloven hooves of pigs, sheep or cattle, which consist of two *clees*

clem *adj.* (also **clammed, clemmed**) 1. famished, starving; 2. hunched or tense with cold

clet *n.* a wedge

clever *adj.* good and right. 'He was always *clever* to me'

clever man *n.* a wizard (S HEREFS)

clibberty *adj.* moist, sticky (particularly of the weather) (NW HEREFS)

clik *n.* a clique or gang

clinker *n.* a hard, burnt brick

clock's upright *n.* noon, midday

clomb *v.* past tense of *clomber.* 'I *clombed* the mountain'

clomber *v.* to climb

close *n.* field. Often used in place-names (e.g. Manor *Close*)

clossen on! come closer. '*Clossen on* so I can see you better'

clot *n.* clod of earth (from the Old English *clott*) (S HEREFS)

clout *n.* 1. a rough patch; 2. a napkin or cloth (a *dish-clout*)

clover-snapper *n.* a rabbit (WIGMORE)

clumbersome *adj.* unwieldy, awkward (a corruption of 'cumbersome') (N HEREFS)

c'mere (also **c'mere a bit, come 'ere back**) instruction to a horse to turn left. See Waggoners' calls, p. 178

coach-roach *n.* the wooden handle or shaft that holds the metal point of the *mill-bill* used for cutting grooves into the surface of a mill stone (in other counties this is called the *thrift*)

cob *n.* 1. a baked apple dumpling; 2. a small, round loaf

cock hoop *n.* (also **hoop**) bullfinch

cockshut *n.* (also **cockshot**) a suspended net for catching woodcocks in an open glade or drive in a wood (also used in place-names)

cod *n.* 1. a pod (pea's pod etc.); 2. the projecting corners of *hop-pockets* are called *cods*

codlin perry *n.* if supplies of cider were exhausted in the summer, cider was sometimes made as a stop-gap from early varieties of culinary apples known as codlins

cofer *n.* corn bin (WIGMORE)

cois *n.* wood pigeon

colin-bill *n.* (also **colinbill**) a hedge bill with the addition of a hook on the back side (ASHPERTON); a long-handled bill-hook (MON BORDER)

collogue *v.* 1. to be friendly. 'Please be *collogue* to him'; 2. to join together (in a bad sense) in league or in conversation. 'They *collogued* and set upon him'

colly *n.*, *adj.* 1. soot from a kettle or pot; 2. black (from 'coal'). 'Scrub the *colly* off that kettle'

collywist *adj.* (also **collwisth'd**) when a ladder does not stand straight on the ground it is said to be *collywist*

come *v.* applied to the increase of a river in flood. 'The Wye's *coming*'

come back! the cry of the guinea fowl

come back here! instruction to horses to turn left. See Waggoners' calls, p. 178

comesnow *n.* ('ow' pronounced as in 'cow') the imminence of snow. 'The clouds are building and it looks like *comesnow*' (MON BORDER)

comical *adj.* cross, peculiar, unwell. 'She's been *comical*'

conceit *v.* to suppose. 'That's what I *conceited*'

condoodle *v.* to get over. 'I'll *condoodle* it in time'

conigree *n.* a rabbit warren (from 'cony'/ 'coney' for rabbit). The word is also used in place-names

consate *v.* to fancy or imagine. 'I *consated* it were so'

contrive *v.* to find out. 'I couldn't *contrive* why he did it' (ARCHENFIELD)

cooch *v.*, *n.* (also **cootch, couch, cutch**) (the 'oo' and 'u' pronounced as the 'u' in 'put') 1. to lie quietly, to settle down, as a restless infant. '*Cooch* down little one'. To lie as one having a kip; to squat or crouch down, including animals (hares etc.); 2. 'to *cooch* away' = to hide away or secrete; 3. a hollow or 'form' where a rabbit or hare *cooches* (settles concealed). The word in these cases derives from the French *coucher* = to put to bed (echoed in the later Welsh *cwtch* = cuddle or hug, offering safety). 4. a safe store; 5. couch grass (sometimes *quich* or *twitch grass*)

cooched on *v.* lying on, lodged on

cooler *n.* 1. a vessel used for cider-making; 2. an oval wooden vessel large enough to take a dead pig for cleaning before salting

coolth *n.* coolness (TENBURY)

coop! coop! call to horses. See Calls to animals, p. 177

cootchy place *n.* a nook, a little retreat. See *cooch*

cooton *n.* (also **cooten, couten, cutten**) ('oo' pronounced as the 'u' in 'put') a dimwit, a fool

cop *n., v., adj.* 1. the top or ridge formed in ploughing; 2. the first bout of ploughing in a field (ASHPERTON); 3. the crest of a ridge; 4. cut, pollarded (probably from the German *kopf* = a head)

cop and lop *n., v.* a felled tree with the top branches cut away; the act of felling and cutting the top branches away

cop and reen *n.* ridge and furrow: the field pattern of ridges and troughs characteristic of medieval ploughing (LEDBURY)

copping out *v.* marking out a field to ensure tidiness and accuracy in ploughing

coppy *n.* a small coppice

cord *n.* (pronounced 'card') a heap of firewood generally measuring 4ft high, 8ft long and 3ft wide. The traditional mode of selling firewood was by the *cord*

cordwood *n.* firewood

corn baby *n.* (also **corn dolly**) a small figure of plaited straw, originally made from part of the final sheaf cut at the end of the harvest, and representing the Corn Spirit on whom the year's crop depended

corney wick *n.* lapwing

cosp *n.* the part of a plough, located on the main beam, that regulates width and depth; the head of the plough

coss *n., v.* (also **cosses**) cost, costs

cossey *n.* (also **cossy, causey**) 1. a causeway or paved walk; 2. a raised walkway around farm buildings (PEMBRIDGE)

cossin *v.* literally coursing, but used in the sense of chasing away rather than in pursuit to capture (as hare coursing). '*Cossin* them off my land!'

costrel *n.* a small portable cask, for beer and cider etc.

cot *n.* a barn for sheep, a sheepfold

cotched *v.*, *adj.* caught. 'He *cotched* a nice brace of rabbits'

cotting *adj.* obstinate, unmanageable

coulter *n.* the part of a plough used for cutting the ground

couse *v.* (also **cowse**) to drive or chase away, particularly sheep and pigs (NW HEREFS)

cousin *n.* a friend. 'They're close *cousins*' (S HEREFS)

coutrements *n.* 1. things strewn about untidily; 2. piles of unwanted stuff (BRAMPTON BRYAN)

cowbanging *v.* tending the cows, e.g. feeding, cleaning out, milking etc. 'He was out *cowbanging* before six this morning' (PEMBRIDGE)

cowt *n.* a colt

cowtyens *n.* upright posts to which cattle are tied in sheds

coxy *adj.* irritable and quarrelsome. 'Keep clear of him when he's tired and *coxy*'

crane *n.* a heron

crank *adj.* clever. 'Watch her, she's a *crank* sort'

cratch *n.*, *v.* 1. a hay rack for cattle, a manger; 2. a rack hanging from the kitchen ceiling for holding flitches of bacon; 3. a hurdle-like frame placed around the top of a waggon to increase its size; 4. the tail-board of a waggon; 5. to eat (of horses and cattle etc.); also to eat heartily, like a horse (of people)

cratcher *n.* one with a good appetite (LEDBURY)

craven *n.* a coward

crazies *n.* buttercups (deriving from the old belief that their scent brought on madness)

cream of the well the first drink of water from a well after midnight on New Year's Eve – the *cream of the well* – traditionally ensured good luck for the coming year

create *v.* to make a fuss; to make a strenuous and wordy objection. Often preceded by the word 'half' used for emphasis. 'He didn't half *create*'

creep *n.* a wooden guard over a small trough enabling lambs to feed while keeping ewes back

creeping buttercup *n.* lesser celandine (plant)

cress *n.* a ridge tile, a crest

crib *n.* a large 'bin', generally comprising canvas or hessian suspended within a raised wooden frame, into which hops were picked in a hopyard

crink *n.* 1. a small, sweet apple or one of stunted growth; 2. a tree producing such fruit; 3. the youngest, smallest or weakest of a litter; also a small or under-grown child; 4. an endearing name for a small animal or child. 'She's a sweet little *crink*'

crips *adj.* crisp. 'It's cold and *crips* out there'

crod *n.* a short, stocky person or beast (BRAMPTON BRYAN)

croodle *v.* to creep close together, to nestle, as chicks under a mother hen

crook-a-down fork *n.* a tool with the prongs or tines bent down, to be used as a hoe or rake

crool *v.*, *adj.* (also **crooly**) to huddle miserably together, e.g. from the cold or wet (BRAMPTON BRYAN)

crop *n.* the lop and top of a felled tree (MON BORDER)

crope *v.* crept (BURFORD, LEINTWARDINE)

crowdle *v.* to crouch or squat. '*Crowdle* down so he won't see you'

crowsty *adj.* (also **crousty, crust**) bad tempered, irritable, morose. 'He's a *crowsty* old bugger' (N HEREFS)

cruddly *adj.* (also **cruddley, cruddledy**) of the sky: a mackerel sky (having clouds in rippling, undulating rows, like fish scales). *Cruddly*, deriving from 'curdled', appears in an old Herefordshire saying: 'A *cruddly* sky means twenty-four hours neither wet nor dry' (MONNOW VALLEY)

cruds *n.* curds

cub *n., v.* 1. a dog kennel, hen coop or rabbit hutch; 2. to confine in a small space. 'I've *cubbed* the hens at the end of the yard' (WIGMORE). Akin to 'cubby hole'

cuck-fist *adj., n.* ham-fisted, awkward-handed

cuckoo lamb *n.* a lamb born out of season

cuckoo oats *n.* oats planted too late (in the 'cuckoo months' of April, May and June)

cuckoo pen *n.* a small and useless enclosure (from an old tale about some people who, to achieve a continuation of summer, erected a pen around a cuckoo) (E HEREFS)

cuckoo-pint *n.* wild arum (plant)

cuckoo's maid *n.* (also **cuckoo's mate**) the curlew, which leaves the coast to nest inland about a week before the cuckoo arrives, 'to get the place ready for the cuckoo'

cues *n., v.* 1. iron plates that were fixed to the hooves of droves of Welsh or Irish cattle for their long journeys to market; 2. to fasten shoes on the feet of oxen

cull *v.* to pick flowers

cullens *n.* (also **cullings**) 1. waste, rejects, as of wheat, apples, potatoes etc.; 2. those animals left in a herd or flock after the best have been selected

cups and saucers *n.* the name given to acorn cups by children

curf *n.*, *v.* (also **kurf, kerf**) 1. a large hoe for earthing up potatoes; 2. to earth up potatoes (LLANGROVE)

curlock *n.* charlock (plant)

cur'ous *adj.* unusual, with a suggestion of ill temper. 'He were ever a *cur'ous* old fellow'

curst *adj.* 1. sharp, clever, especially referring to mischief. 'His younger brother's a *curst* little devil'; 2. ill-tempered (of man or beast)

cushat *n.* collared dove

cusp *n.* (also **cosp**) 1. a tooth; 2. part of the front of a plough to which the whippletrees were hooked, used to regulate the width of furrows

cussing the cook a ploughman is said to be *cussing the cook* when his plough wheel squeaks for want of grease

custish *adj.*, *adv.* sharpish. 'You best go and get those sheep in *custish*'

cut *adj.* drunk (ROSS). See *chemist*

cute *adj.* (also **cude**) sharp, acrimonious

cutten *adj.*, *v.*, *n.* (also **cooten**) 1. cut, to cut. 'I've *cutten* my finger'; 2. a simpleton, a fool (ROSS, N HEREFS)

cutwith *n.* the plough bar to which the traces are attached

cyder wring *n.* a cider press

D

dabbledy *adj.* (also **dabbley, dabbly, draggly**) very showery; fine for only short periods between the rain (ORCOP)

dacky *n.* a small pig (WIGMORE)

daddiky *adj.* (also **daddocky, droxy**) 1. chiefly of wood, rotten or beginning to rot and become tindery, having lost its dure; unsound (*daddock* from 'dead oak'); 2. soft, rotten (of fruit etc.); 3. said of people with aches and pains (MON BORDER)

daddle *n.*, *v.* a stroll; to go for a stroll. 'He's just popped out for a short *daddle*' (GOLDEN VALLEY)

daffidowndilly *n.* (also **daffydowndilly**) daffodil. *Daffydowndilly* appears in a traditional nursery rhyme from the nineteenth century. It also appears in a short story (*Little Daffydowndilly*) by American writer Nathaniel Hawthorne (1804–64) published in 1887

daffish *adj.* 1. bashful, shy, embarrassed (ROSS); 2. full of aches and pains (MON BORDER)

dahnt *v.*, *adj.* (also **dahnted**) to daunt, dishearten; daunted, disheartened, low-spirited, nonplussed

daim *v.* consider, deem. 'I *daim* it'll rain yet' (S HEREFS)

dall it! (also **danker it!**, **dauze it!**) damn it! confound it!

dammock *v.* (also **dommock**) to dirty or soil clothes. 'She isn't one to *dammock* her clothes' (NW HEREFS)

dandering *v.*, *adj.* talking nonsense, *twaddling*

dannies *n.* (also **dandies**) a baby's hands. 'Clap your *dannies*' (N HEREFS, GOLDEN VALLEY)

dap *v.* 1. to bounce; 2. to beat, to cane; 3. to press into ones hand; to offer a tip. 'He *dapped* me sixpence' (S HEREFS)

daps *n.* plimsolls (ROSS)

dar *n.* a mark, for example as set up in a field to measure by

dark *adj.* 1. heavily shaded. A '*dark* orchard' is one in which the trees are crowded together; 2. blind

darter *n.* (also **dahter**) daughter

dashed *adj.* abashed, embarrassed

daunting *adj.* (of illness, pain etc.) tiresome, depressing

dawny *adj.* (also **dawney**) 1. damp (particularly with dew and applied to grain), dank (N HEREFS); 2. untrustworthy or dishonest

day-house *n.* dairy

dazzed *adj.*, *v.* flummoxed, stupefied. 'It right *dazzed* me'

dead *adj.* 1. unconscious, in a faint. 'I knocked myself out and was *dead* for a while'; 2. 'Ringing home the *dead*' = ringing the church bells as the funeral procession nears the church, then changing to tolling a bell as it enters the churchyard (N HEREFS)

dead alive *adj.* very stupid

deadman *n.* a scarecrow (ROSS)

dearn *adj.* (also **diern**) (sometimes pronounced 'jearn') severe, hard, dour, strict, stern. Usually applied to men, but also applied to raw or cold weather, e.g. 'a *diern* frost'

deathzear *n.* the twelve months following a death in the family (N HEREFS)

deawbeater *n.* a person who walks with their toes very much turned out

deawbit *n.* slight early refreshment

deed *adv.* indeed

deedily *adv.* earnestly (S HEREFS)

deedy *adj.* 1. bustling, stirring; 2. a '*deedy* conversation' is one in which the talkers are so absorbed that they are oblivious to all else (ROSS)

deef *adj.* deaf

deepness *n.*, *adj.* cunning, sly. 'She's full of *deepness*'

denial *n.* disadvantage, injury (the loss of a limb or faculty is spoken of as 'a great *denial*')

dergy *adj.* (pronounced with a hard 'g') short and thick-set

desacly *adv.* exactly. 'It's *desacly* what I wanted'

despert *adv.*, *adj.* (also **desperate**) extremely, very

deuced *adv.*, *adj.* (also **deeowsid, djouced**) very (used for emphasis) 'I'm *deuced* unhappy about it'

devil *n.* (also **cider devil, muller**) a cornet-shaped copper or tin container used for heating cider

devil screamer *n.* (also **devil-screecher, devilin**) the swift (bird), from its distinctive 'screaming' cry

devil's garden *n.* one in which nothing grows (KINGTON)

devil's guts *n.* common elder, goutweed

devil's rings *n.* hairy caterpillars (NW HEREFS)

devil's snuffbox *n.* a puff-ball (fungus)

devildom *adj.* devilish. 'Those *devildom* kids!'

dewing *n.* (also **duewing**) small rain, mizzle. 'It's only *dewing* but take a coat anyway' (UPPER SAPEY)

didapper *n.* little grebe (bird)

diddikoy *n.* gypsy. 'Dadika' was originally a respectful Romani term for an older person; however, the word was later misappropriated as a term of abuse for a gypsy not of 'pure' (Romani) blood, thus with the negative associations of being both a vagrant and being of questionable descent

dilly *n.* (also **dilbury**) an epithet for almost any kind of open, wheeled vehicle (cart etc.), not hand-propelled, though most commonly refers to a light, narrow-wheeled dray (BRAMPTON BRYAN). Also used disparagingly to refer to a car. 'Look at his rusty old *dilly*!' (ROSS)

dilly! dilly! dilly! (also **dil! dil!**) call to geese. See Calls to animals, p. 177

diou! diou! a call to pigs. See Calls to animals, p. 177

dip *adj.* deep

dipping *v.* 'counting out' in children's games

disaccord *v.* to disagree. 'I strongly *disaccord* with you'

disburst *v.* to disburse. 'After the fight they all *disbursted*'

disfuglement *n.* disfigurement

disgest *v.* to digest

dish-clout *n.* a dish-cloth

dishabils *n.* a woman's working clothes. From the French *déshabiller* = to undress

dishwasher *n.* pied or 'water' wagtail (bird)

dither *n.*, *v.* 1. a confused noise; bother; 2. to tremble, shake

dithering *adj.* (also **dithery**) shaky, confused, trembling 'He's a *dithering* old man' (W HEREFS)

divvy duck *n.* applied generally to diving ducks or water birds, but especially to little grebe, moorhen and mallard

djern *adj.* (also **dearn, djurn, jern, journ, jurn**) 1. eager, keen, determined (N HEREFS, EARDISLAND); 2. hard, severe, stern, surly (LEDBURY, ROWLSTONE). See *dearn*

djud *adj.* (also **dyud**) dead

do *v.* used as an auxiliary verb for emphasis, to express an affirmative or a habit. 'I *do* say'; I *do* be at work mostly'

dobbin *n*. 'That's just my *dobbin*' = that suits me well
doddering dillies *n*. quaking grass
d'off *v*. to do off or put off (clothes, thus to *d'off* one's cap)
doglogarum *n*. nonsense. 'What a load of *doglogarum*'
doit *n*. a small coin
dolent *adj*. 1. sharp and clever; 2. conversely, *dolent* can mean docile (SUTTON ST NICHOLAS)
dolly *n*. an implement used for washing clothes in a wash tub, made of timber and comprising a shaft with a crossways handle at the top, and several (typically six) radiating legs at the bottom. It would be pushed into the washing and twisted back and forth to clean the clothes (ASHPERTON)
doncass *v*. to behave inelegantly. 'She's been *doncassing* after the young men'
done *adj*. nonplussed, confounded. 'I'm totally *done* by it'
donkey's beans *n*. thistles (N HEREFS)
donnings *n*. fine clothes. 'He's lording it in his *donnings*'
doos *v*. does. Used, for example, instead of the phrase 'does do'. 'He *doos* it' = he does do it
dormant *adj*. ill in bed, confined to bed
dormedory *n*. a sleepy, stupid person who does not work
dormit *n*. an attic or dormer window
dotey *adj*. rotten, soft (e.g. of fruit, wood etc.)
dother *n*. (also **duthering**) a din or confusion
double dwelling *n*. a semi-detached house (KINGSTONE)
double lambs *n*. twin lambs
doubles *n*. 1. a bent state of the body. 'I was down in my *doubles*'; 2. twin lambs

doubt *v.* expect, think, perceive that; used in the opposite sense to the ordinary meaning. 'I *doubt* it will' = I'm confident it will

douce *n.* a blow on the face (ORLETON)

douk *v.* (pronounced 'daouk') to lower or duck one's head. It was believed that ducks lowered their heads when flying through e.g. a barn door, hence the term

doust *n.*, *adj.*, *v.* (also **dousty**) 1. dust; 2. dusty; 3. to put out, harm, destroy. 'That blow to his head near *dousted* him'

dout *v.* 1. to put out, extinguish (e.g. a candle); 2. 'He just *douted*' = he just died; he quietly passed away

douting out *v.* making rows for potatoes (W HEREFS)

dowe *n.* ('dowe' to rhyme with 'how') (also **doo, doe**) dove

downhill *adj.* applied to wind from the south

draft *n.* a joint (of pork)

drag *n.* a fence placed across running water, consisting of a kind of hurdle which swings on hinges, fastened to a horizontal pole. See *argy*

draggletail *n.* a dress trailing on the ground. 'She's gone off to church in her *draggletail*'

drave *n.* (also **thrave**) 24 boltings of straw

draw down to an expression used to describe an unhurried, steady approach. 'We *drew down to* the brook'. Probably from sheep-handling usage

drawt *n.* the spring balance of a clock (BRAMPTON BRYAN)

dreaten *v.* to threaten

drench *v.*, *n.* to pour or force liquid (medicine etc.) down an animal's throat; to force to drink a large quantity

dresh *v.* (also **thrash**) to thresh (N HEREFS)

dreshel *n.* (also **drashel, threshel**) a flail (the substitution of 'd' for 'th' is common in Herefordshire) (N HEREFS)
drills *n.* a sow's teats
drip *n.* (also **grip**) a rut or little open road-drain (PIXLEY)
dripping bags *n.* bags of canvas like inverted sugar cones through which cider is passed fresh from the cider press
dripples *n.* slatted extensions to the side of a waggon to increase its capacity (for e.g. hay etc.). See *thripples*
drop out *v.* to fall out, to quarrel
dropping night *n.* (also **drop night**) a late dusk, nightfall. See *edge of night*
droughty *adj.* thirsty. 'I'm famished and *droughty*'
drow *v.* to throw
droxy *adj.* soft or rotten. See *daddiky*
druft *n.*, *adj.* drought; a *drufty* wind = a warm drying wind
druv *adj.* driven
dry scrubber *n.* a hammer (facetious)
dryth *n.* dryness
duberous *v.*, *adj.* 1. to bend or pull down; 2. doubtful
duff *n.*, *adj.*, *adv.* 1. the sound of the impact of a generally soft object (onomatopoeic); 2. to 'fall *duff*' is to fall hard; 3. directly, full. 'The ball struck him *duff* on the mouth'
dumb-cake *n.* 'a small cake made and baked in complete silence on Halloween [31 October] or St Agnes Eve [21 January] by girls who wanted to know if they would be married during the coming year. It consisted of an egg-spoonful of salt, flour and water (sometimes other ingredients as well) mixed and baked over a fire. On retiring for the night, the girl placed it under a pillow,

or, alternatively, ate it, and then hoped to dream of a young man – a good sign for marriage' (WL)

dumb-saucy *adj.* sulky. 'Don't get all *dumb-saucy* about it' (SUTTON ST NICHOLAS)

dumble-hole *n.* a derelict clay pit or quarry (N HEREFS)

dummel *n.* a stupid creature

dunch *adv.*, *v.* 1. heavily (of a blow or strike). 'It hit him *dunch*'; 2. to poke against something (*dunching* = poking)

dunchy *adj.* variant of *lunchy*; of wet, heavy soil

dung-heavle *n.* a dung-fork

dunna *v.* negative of 'does': does not. 'He *dunna* have the money for it'

dunnick *n.* (also **dunnock**) 1. a heap; 2. a dung fork (N & W HEREFS)

dunnot 1. don't; 2. dare not. 'I *dunnot* go in there'

dunny *adj.* 1. stupid (ROSS); 2. deaf, hard of hearing (AYLTON)

dup *v.* to do up, to fasten. 'Go and *dup* your laces'

dure *n.*, *v.* 1. of wood, lasting strength, endurance; 2. to endure generally

duther *v.* 1. to annoy, bother; 2. to confuse, bewilder

duthery *adj.* shivery, shaky (with cold or fear)

dwaddle *n.* nonsense, twaddle

dwarf money *n.* old coins turned up in ploughing (KENCHESTER, W HEREFS)

dwu dwu! dear dear! (RADNOR BORDER)

dyche *n.* a mound, the bank of a hedge, a dyke

dyson *n.* the flax or fibres on a distaff (an implement for spinning)

E

ean *v.*, *adj.* (also **een, yean**) of a ewe, to give birth; to lamb. A ewe is said to be '*in ean*' when in lamb

eaning time *n.* (also **yeaning time**) the lambing season

eariwig *n.* earwig

earthly *adj.* near death. 'Dear me, how *earthly* she looks'

ease aya fust! instruction to horses to move forward (E HEREFS). See Waggoners' calls, p. 178

easement *n.* relief, respite. 'My pills give me some *easement*'

edder *n.* adder (BREDWARDINE)

edge of night *n.* dusk. 'Make sure you're back before *edge of night*' (N & E HEREFS)

eelrake *n.* (also **ell-rake**) a form of heel rake (a wide rake of triangular form with long tines for raking hay); also more generally a hayfork (WIGMORE)

eequaw *n.* (also **eacle, equal, equaw, eqwal, hecle, hickol**) green woodpecker; occasionally refers to a magpie

effet *n.* (also **evvet**) newt (LINGEN)

eft *n.* 1. in one's own way or time. 'He did it at his own *eft*'. 'Any *eft*' = any quantity or amount

eggs and bacon *n.* yellow toadflax (plant)

eimer *adj.* (also **eemer, eemest**) near, nearest way (N HEREFS)

elder *n.* a cow's udder (N HEREFS)

ellern *n.* (also **ellan**) elderberry tree

ellern blows *n.* ('blows' pronounced as in 'cows') elderberry blossom

ellum *n.*, *adj.* (also **elmen**) elm tree; made of elm

emmets *n.* ants (S HEREFS)

empt *v.* 1. to pour out, to empty; 2. to pour with rain. 'The rain *empts* down'

enna *v.* am not. 'I *enna* happy' (N HEREFS)

ent *v.* (also **yent**) ain't, is not; isn't it? 'It is yours *ent*?'

er *pron.* he, she, it. '*Er*'s an idiot'; '*Er*'s raining hard'

erriwig *n.* earwig

errun *n.* a single one, even one. 'Haven't you got *errun*?'

espel *v.* (also **hespel**) to harass, worry, annoy (N HEREFS)

esplin *v.* to hinder (WIGMORE)

ess *n.* ashes. 'I've swept the *ess* from the hearth' (AYLTON)

etherings *n.* (also **heatherings**) long stakes of oak or willow, or rods of hazel, used in pleaching hedges

ett! to a horse, an instruction to turn right

ettles *n.* (also **ettleys**) nettles

ever *n.* (also **hever**) hemlock (plant)

ever so 1. in any case. 'He's not going your way, *ever so*'; 2. on no account (used in the negative)

evvet *n.* newt (GOLDEN VALLEY)

exempt *adj.* without a crop. 'I'm *exempt* of plums this year'

ey-ah! (also **ey-ah boy!**) call to one's dog. See Calls to animals, p. 177

eye *n.* the central spot, the main place, as in the old saying: 'Blessed is the *eye* / That's between Severn and Wye'

F

face *n.* surface. 'That field has a fine *face*' (S HEREFS)

fadge *v.* 'To *fadge* it' = to go on or proceed

fagging hook *n.* (also **faggot hook**) like a bill hook but with a slightly curved point

faggot *n.* (also **fagget, faggit**) a derogatory word applied to a woman or ill-behaved girl. Also a term of reproach used of emaciated old people (from *faggot* as a bundle of sticks, thus akin to a 'bag of bones')

fainty *adj.* a weak or faint state

fair to middling *adj.* (of health) so-so, not too good

fairises *n.* fairies

fairy darts *n.* flint arrowheads turned up by ploughing

fairy gloves *n.* foxgloves (KENTCHURCH)

fairy money *n.* old coins turned up by ploughing. See *dwarf money*

faldigo-lay *adj., n.* bone lazy; a lazy fellow. 'A useless *faldigo-lay* who never lifted a finger' (GOLDEN VALLEY)

fall *v., n.* 1. to fell (a tree); 2. an area of woodland set aside for felling; 3. to throw down generally

falling weather *n.* when rain or snow may be expected

fancical *adj.* fanciful

fangles *n.* the teeth or tines of a fork (like fangs)

fantigue *n.* excitement. 'There was great *fantigue* at their arrival'

farden-piece *n.* farthing

fat hen *n.* the farmland 'weed', *Chenopodium alba.* Also known as white goosefoot and lamb's quarters

fatch *n.* thatch

fatches *n.* vetches (members of the pea family)

favour *v.* to bear lightly on, to ease from pressure, as a horse may. 'He *favours* his right leg'

fear *v.* to frighten. 'The sight of it *feared* me greatly'

fearn *n.* (also **feern, fiern, vearn**) bracken

feather *v.* 1. to pluck poultry; 2. 'The old woman is *feathering* her goose' = it's snowing

featherfold *n.* the herb feverfew (the aromatic, daisy-like flowering perennial, *Tanacetum parthenium*)

feature *v.* to resemble, as an ancestor. 'They *feature* one another like two peas' (W HEREFS)

feed *v.* to grow fat. 'He's eating well and *feeding*'

feg *n.* (also **fag**) long, rough, coarse grass; grass that has withered on the ground without being cut

fellon *n.* (also **fellom, felon**) a whitlow (an infection of the finger); an inflammation on the hand more generally

fellow *n.* 1. one of a pair ('the *fellow* sock'); 2. a servant employed in animal husbandry; 3. a young unmarried man

feltyfare *n.* (also **felt, fildefare**) fieldfare (bird)

feo *n., adj.* (also **feow**) few (SE HEREFS)

fer *adv., adj.* (also **fur, vur**) far

fern *n.* a large number. 'A *fern* of crows' (LEDBURY)

fern-owl *n.* (also **fiern-owl**) nightjar (also known by the vernacular name *goat-sucker*)

ferretting and brevitting *v.* rummaging, fossicking, searching about. 'She's in the pantry *ferretting and brevitting*' (PEMBRIDGE)

fetch *v.* 1. to deal a blow. 'He *fetched* me about the head'; 2. to make butter by churning ('to *fetch* butter')

fetlock *n.* as well as being a lower leg joint of e.g. a horse, the word appears in the phrase: 'To catch the day by the *fetlock*' = to be up early; to seize the opportunity (W HEREFS)

fettle *v.* to feed or '*ed up*' cattle; to set in proper order

fickeldy *adj.* fickle (ARCHENFIELD)

fiddle *n.* a fiddle-shaped box from which seeds were scattered during sowing

fiddle-faddle *v.* to potter about aimlessly

fidge *n., v.* (also **fizzle**) a fidget, especially a child; the wriggling or twisting about of a child expected to sit still

field-dressing *v.* (also **meadow-dressing**) the levelling out of molehills before the start of hay-making. This was a task traditionally performed by women (N HEREFS)

fild *n.* field

filler *n.* (also **fill horse**) shaft horse

filler gears *n.* (also **viller**) for a shaft or filler horse: collar and *hames* with tugs, cart-saddle, crupper and britching

filthy *adj.* (also **viltry**) used specifically for 1. a field full of weeds ('a *filthy* field'); 2. a person with lice

fimble *n.* a chimney made of wattle and daub (a woven lattice of sticks daubed with e.g. clay, animal dung etc.)

finegue *v.* to avoid or evade something. 'He left early and *finegued* paying' = avoided paying

firebrand tail *n.* (also **brandtail**) redstart (bird) (MONNOW VALLEY, SUTTON ST NICHOLAS)

fireweed *n.* used for several fleshy-leaved plants (including sorrel, field scabious and plantain) which, when cut in hay, do not dry easily and cause the rick to heat and become *mow-burned* (KENTCHURCH)

firm *v.* to affirm. 'He *firmed* it were so'

fit *n.* feet

fitchet *n.* (also **fitchett, fitchock, fitchuck**) variously used for a polecat, stoat or ferret

fither *v.* (also **futher**) to fiddle about (*fithering* = fiddling)
fitmeal *adv.* in fits; piecemeal. 'He built the shed *fitmeal*'
fittle *n.* victual, food, provisions
flabber *v., n.* (also **flaw, flawn**) to whip up, stir up, lather (LEOMINSTER). *Flawn* comes from an Old English word meaning custard. A child trying to blow bubbles was told to '*flabber* the suds up and make a *flaw*' = stir up the suds and make a lather (WL)
flail *n.* 1. a *threshel* for separating grain from husks, made up of a *handstaff* (the part held by the workman), a *nile*, *swingel* or *pelt* (the part swung round and beaten against the straw) and a *capling* or *thonk* (which joins the *nile* to the *handstaff*); 2. a basket originally woven from rushes, but later made of canvas, in which workmen carried their food or tools
flannen *n.* flannel, wool (from *gwlanen*, the Welsh word for flannel, itself derived from *gwlan*, wool)
flat *n.* a hollow in a field
flath *n.* dirt, filth, ordure. 'Go and wash off that *flath*'
fleak *n.* (also **flake**) a hurdle
fleam *n.* phlegm
fleamy *adj.* loose, as a cough
fled *v.* past tense of 'to fly'. 'The gate *fled* open'
flen *v., n.* (also **flem**) 1. to flay; 2. fleas (N HEREFS)
flence *v.* to flinch. 'He *flenced* when I raised my hand'
flickets *n.* (also **fluckets**) rags and tatters. 'She was clad all in *flickets*' (ROSS)
flidgeter *n.* a flying leap. 'He took a *flidgeter*' (W HEREFS)
flit *v.* to move house

flitchen *n.* a flitch of bacon (a side of bacon that has been salted and cured)

flizz *v.* to break or fly in pieces

floatsome *n.*, *adj.* a corruption of 'flotsam'; timber carried downriver by a flood

floor *v.* to fell a tree

flopperty *adj.*, *adv.* slack, limp, floppy; floppily. 'She went all *flopperty* and fainted'

flotch *n.* a trapdoor set into a larger door, as in a chicken house. 'Shut and latch the *flotch*' (S HEREFS)

flowering *v.* 1. to go *flowering* = to gather wild flowers; 2. *flowering* the graves = decorating graves with flowers on *Flowering Sunday*, for the Festival of the Resurrection (Palm or Easter Sunday)

fluish *adj.* weak of mind (traditionally applied to women)

flummock *n.* a slovenly person. 'He's a lazy *flummock*'

flummocks *v.* to maul, to mangle. 'I saw the fox *flummocks* the hens'

flump *n.*, *v.*, *adv.*, *adj.* 1. a heavy fall; 2. to fall heavily; 3. 'I fell down *flump*'; 4. plump

flush *n.*, *adj.* 1. a rush of water; 2. fledged (applied to birds) (MON BORDER)

flusher *n.* red-backed shrike (bird)

fluttermouse *n.* bat (N HEREFS)

fly *v.*, *n.* break, split, splinter, crack, chip or other breakage by violence; to fly to pieces. Generally applied to metal (a split water pipe might be said to have '*fled* in the frost')

ford *n.* place-names terminating thus are pronounced 'fut'. Thus: Hereford = Here*fut*; Mordiford = Mordi*fut* etc.

forehanded pay *n.* a payment in advance (S HEREFS)
forrat *v., adj.* forward, to bring forward. 'These showers will *forrat* the hay'
foul *n.* a disease of the foot in cattle
fould *n.* (also **fauld**) fold; the fold yard
fowsty *adj.* (also **fousty, frowsty**) fusty, mouldy. A room long shut up might smell *fousty* (PEMBRIDGE)
frail *n.* (also **frale**) 1. a light rush basket; 2. an open shopping basket; 3. a workman's tool bag
fratchy *adj.* (also **frangy, frant, frany, fretchy, fretchity, fretchet**) fretful, irritable, violent-tempered, fractious, restive, fidgety (W HEREFS)
fraturn *v.* to echo or reflect, expressive of facial likeness in siblings. 'She *fraturns* her sister' = she looks like her sister
free-martin *n.* when a cow gives birth to twin calves, both females, one is believed always to be barren, and is called a *free-martin* (ASHPERTON)
frem *adj.* fresh, chilly (as early morning air). 'It's cool and *frem* out this morning' (FOWNHOPE)
french eagle *n.* green woodpecker
fresh *v., adj.* 1. of e.g. cattle, starting to show signs of better keep. 'At last he's got those cows *fresh*'; 2. a little drunk; excited but not yet intoxicated by alcohol
fresh liquor *n.* unsalted hog's lard
fret *v.* to ferment. 'The cider's *fretting* nicely in its cask'
fretchett *adj.* fretful
frighten *v.* to conquer or get through a piece of work. 'She's *frightened* that tricky job'
frightful *adj.* easily frightened, jumpy

frit *adj.* (also **fritful**) frightened, timorous

from *adv.* away from. 'You must get *from* here by sundown'

fromward *adv.* from, but suggestive of dynamic movement from one direction. 'That wind's *fromward* the north'

frosted *adj.* frozen

frowardly *adj., adv.* a corruption of 'forwardly'; confidently, forthrightly

fruit *n.* apples specifically (the fruit of the county)

frum *adj.* (also **frummest**) 1. early, out of season (e.g. *frum* potatoes are early potatoes); 2. forward, well-grown, as fruit, hops etc. (the *frummest* hops); early and luxuriant in vegetation more generally; 3. tender or brittle

frumenty *n.* (also **furmenty, furmity**) wheat boiled with milk (a Whit Sunday breakfast dish) (W HEREFS)

fuddle *v., n.* to potter; a muddle. 'Shop-window *fuddle*' = window-shopping (LEOMINSTER)

fullaring *n.* the groove in a horseshoe

full of *n.* an amount by comparison; capacity. 'The *full of* that waggon is about a ton'

fume *v.* 1. to become inflamed, particularly as a wound (STAUNTON-ON-WYE); 2. to get in a passion

fund *v.* found. 'I *fund* it under the table'

furness *n.* distance (a corruption of 'farness')

furze-chat *n.* whinchat (bird). *Furze* = gorse

fusling iron *n.* a gun (from the French *fusil*)

fut *n.* (also **fit**) foot, feet

futher *v.* to fiddle about, to try this and that; hounds *futhering* (or *feathering*) are searching for a scent

G

gadaman *adj.* roguish. 'He was a *gadaman* sort of lad'

gadding *v.* (of cattle) rushing about, tormented by gadflies

gain *adj.* 1. workmanlike, handy; 2. nearer, more convenient

gainest *adj.* the most profitable or best way of carrying out a task or doing something

gale *v.* in mining, to *gale* a mine is to acquire the right to work a mine. See *gaveller*

galeeny *n.* 1. a guinea fowl (from the Latin *gallina* = hen); 2. a fool (BRAMPTON BRYAN)

gall *n.* (also **gaul**) a spring in a field

gallier *n.* (also **hallier**) one who keeps teams for hire

gallous *adj.* 1. (also **gallus**) high-spirited, mischievous (applied to children or animals); 2. fit for the gallows

gally *adj.* wet, sodden, as applied to land. 'The bottom field was always too *gally* to sow'

gally-team *n.* a team (of workers) kept for hire

gambo *n.* (also **gamber, gambrel**) a farm cart with no front or back, with sides only (ROWLESTONE, N HEREFS)

gambol *v.* to climb (over a stile) (N HEREFS)

gambrel *n.* (also **gamble**) 1. the wooden bar from which carcasses are hung for butchering; 2. a cart with rails

ganzey *n.* a high-necked jersey (STOKE EDITH)

gapesing *v., adj.* sightseeing, looking around. 'We went up to London for a spot of *gapesing*'

gather *v.* to plough so that the furrows fall inwards towards each other, so as to form a *top* or gathering

gaum! *n., v.* (also **bygamm, gams**) 1. an exclamation, akin to 'by God!': 'By *gaum*, that's tasty!'; 2. to stuff and gorge

gaumed *adj.* (also **gawmed**) 1. thickly covered in grease, clogged with dirt; 2. stupid

gaun *n.* 1. a wooden container with a handle on one side, used for carrying the juice in cider-making; 2. a small wooden ladle or bucket holding about one gallon

gaveller *n.* an officer from whom permission to work a mine may be sought

gawby *n.* a simpleton

gawk *adj.*, *n.* 1. awkward (N HEREFS); 2. an awkward person

gawkey *n.* a gaping idler; one who stands and stares

gawm *v.*, *n.* 1. to smear thickly, as with grease; 2. a gallon

gay *adj.* in good order; well provided for

gear *v.*, *n.* (also **geer**) 1. to harness a horse, to put *gears* on him; 2. a harness, typically for a working horse. See *filler gears*, *gee-o-gears*, *long gears*, *short gears*

geat *n.* gate

gee-back! (also **gee!**) to a horse, command to turn right. See Waggoners' calls, p. 178

gee-o-gears *n.* harness: collar and *hames*, backband and traces with a *battakin*

gee-o-lines *n.* thin reins, usually of cotton rope and tapered, used in harnesses (particularly ploughing gears) (E HEREFS)

gee-o-tack *v.* to plough with two horses abreast

geld *v.* 1. used to describe taking the top off something. 'To *geld anty tumps*' = to take the tops off ant-hills; 2. to castrate (e.g. a horse, thus 'gelding')

get beyond *v.* (pronounced 'beyand') to recover, cure or control. 'Good to see you *get beyond* your cold'

get by! get out of my way!

get less *v.* literally to diminish, but generally used as a euphemism for pilfering. 'You best bolt your store unless you want to *get less*'

get the turn *v.* to be past the crisis in an illness. 'She was very ill, but has *got the turn* now'. See *get beyond*

gewel *v.* (pronounced with a hard 'g') to keep an unsteady course, to wander, to *wame*

gib *n.* a male cat, castrated

gidderskins *v., adj.* playing about, 'on the spree'. 'I'm off *gidderskins* this weekend' (N HEREFS)

gifts *n.* white specks on finger nails, which supposedly foretell the arrival of a gift

gifture *n.* a gift or present. The word is found in the expression: 'I wouldn't have it for a *gifture*', meaning I wouldn't want it even as a gift

giglet *n.* (also **giglot**) a skittish young woman, a giddy girl, a laughing girl (ROSS) (*giglot* is Shakespearean)

gigleting *v.* giggling. 'Look at the pair of them *gigleting*'

gillies *n.* wallflowers

gilling *n.* a salmon of 7lb to 12lb; a term more common on the Severn than on the Wye. See *botcher*

gin *v.* (pronounced with a hard 'g') to give. 'I *gin* it him'

ginny rings *n.* iron rings hitching two horses to two poles

glat *n., v.* 1. a gap in a hedge; 2. to mend gaps in a hedge. 'He's *glatting* up in the top field'

glean *v.* to lease corn

glemmy *adj.* of the weather: close, hot and oppressive, as before a thunder storm, thundery (N HEREFS). See *puthery*

glore *adj.* used as a superlative, specifically relating to fat or fire. 'That's a *glore* blaze you got going there!' (ORLETON)

gnats flying over *n.* a phrase used to denote a slight drizzle. 'Leave your hat, it's just *gnats flying over*' (MUCH MARCLE)

goat sucker *n.* nightjar (bird)

gobbet *n.* (also **gobbit**) a small piece, a mouthful

gobbies' corner *n.* boys' or a gang's meeting place (WIGMORE)

golden chain tree *n.* laburnum

gollup *v.* (also **gullup**) to gulp

gompassing *v.* (also **gompussing about**) 1. gallivanting about (LLANWARNE); 2. roaming or travelling about for pleasure. 'I spent a happy week *gompassing* in the hills'

gone dead *v., adj.* in effect, lifeless to me. 'He's been away so long he's *gone dead*' (W HEREFS)

good evening greeting used at any time after midday

good neighbourhood *n.* amicable relations; mutual help

good-sorted *adj.* 1. kind, generous; 2. of a good type. 'Those Pippins are *good-sorted* apples'

gooding day *n.* it was customary for the poor to visit farmhouses for gifts of wheat on St Thomas' Day (21 Dec). A quartern measure was the quantity traditionally given to each applicant

goosmachick *n.* (also **goosemachick**) gosling (N HEREFS)

gore *n.* 1. a triangular piece of land; 2. a small strip of land lying between two larger pieces. *Gore* often appears in place-names (e.g. *Gore* Farm, The Old *Gore*, etc.). From the Old English word *gara* = an angular piece of land (SE HEREFS)

gorm *v.* according to FH, to *gorm* is to make less dirty; however, according to GCL, to *gorm* is to smear or to make dirty. The etymology supports the latter (the Saxon word *gor* = mire); however, the former may be a variant usage

gornal *n.* a fool (N HEREFS)

gorrells *n.* young pigs

gorse bird *n.* stonechat

gorstly *adj.* (also **gorsty**) abounding in gorse

gorsty piece *n.* a field or area full of gorse bushes

goslings *n.* 1. pussy willow; 2. a patient recovering from an illness might be termed 'as useless as a midsummer *gosling*' (goslings were believed to go weak and stagger about in the sun) (W HEREFS)

gospel oak *n.* a tree on a parish boundary, beneath which the priest read the Gospel during the parochial round

gossips *n.* godparents, sponsors (ARCHENFIELD)

got *v.* meaning 'become', but used after, rather than before, the adjective. 'It's very rainy *got*'

gout *n.* a short trench by the side of the road, a conduit; a drain from a house (from the French *égout* = sewer)

gownd *n.* a gown

grab *n.* crab apple

graft *n.*, *v.* (also **graff**) 1. a long narrow tool or spade for digging, specifically for cutting a drain (BREDWARDINE, WIGMORE); 2. a spade depth; 3. to dig with a spade

grancher *n.* (also **grandfer**) grandfather

granny reared *adj.* 1. over-indulged, spoilt; 2. illegitimate (WIGMORE)

granny's bonnets *n.* columbine (plant)

granny's gown *n.* fumitory (plant)
granny's pincushions *n.* scabious (plant) (MON BORDER)
grass hook *n.* a hook or scythe with a cranked handle (LEDBURY)
grass nail *n.* a part of a scythe, hooked at one end, which passes through a hole in the blade and through the lower ring at the other end, and controls the angle of the blade
graves *n.* the waste remaining at the bottom of the melting pot used to make tallow candles was collected and pressed into oblong cakes. This waste was called *graves*, and was generally boiled with water as dog food
great *adj.*, *v.* (pronounced 'greet') familiar, intimate with. 'He's been *great* with her a while now'
green meat *n.* clover or vetches, cut green and fed to horses
greenstone *n.* name given to the soft slaty rocks found on the Radnorshire border
grig one's teeth *v.* to grit one's teeth (W HEREFS)
grip *n.*, *v.* 1. a small trench or gutter, such as is cut in a roadside verge to carry off surface water; 2. to *grip* = to make or dig a trench or gutter
groanin *n.* a confinement; the final stages of a pregnancy
groats *n.* oats that have been hulled but not ground
grooly *adj.* in a bad, damp, dilapidated condition; slummy or tumbledown (of houses, farm buildings etc.)
growing moon *n.* 1. the waxing moon: the period that aids growth; 2. an auspicious time to take on the running of a farm (W HEREFS)
growing weather *n.* weather that is warm and wet
grub *n.* a caterpillar

gryze *n.*, *v.* 1. a mark or abrasion; 2. to *gryze* is to squeeze or abrade, rub etc. (a corruption of *graze*)

gubban hole *n.* (also **gubbin hole**) a cesspit or rubbish pit

gubbins *n.* rubbish, junk, flotsam

gule *v.* (also **gewl**) 1. to gaze about aimlessly; 2. to pry; 3. to laugh; 4. to glory or boast; 5. to make fun of (*guling*)

gull *n.* (also **gullets**) 1. a gosling; 2. a catkin

gurgeons *n.* pollard (a fine bran containing some flour)

gurly *adj.* stormy, rough, tempestuous (of the weather)

guss *n.* girth. 'That oak's a fine tree with a huge *guss*'

guttie *n.* a disease in cattle

gwaine *v.* (also **gwaying**, **gwine**, **gwy'in**) going

gwammel *n.* a white elephant; a useless thing (N HEREFS)

gwarrell *n.* (also **gweddel**, **gwerrel**, **gwethal**, **gwethel**) accumulated trash, rubbish, something of no value; household stuff (denoting a collection of material). From the Welsh *gweddill* = remnants (N & W HEREFS)

gwerit *n.* bogey man; a ghost or spirit (N HEREFS)

gwilly *n.* bed. 'I'm off up to *gwilly*' (NE HEREFS)

H

hackasing *v.* playing the fool (LYONSHALL)

hacker *n.* 1. a mattock; 2. a bill- or hedge-hook

hackle *n.* a conical thatch for beehives; sheaves inverted and spread to form the top covering of a stack of corn

haggle *v.*, *adj.* 1. to argue; 2. to harass, worry; 3. to struggle against the odds. 'He had to *haggle* it out'; 4. to make difficulties. 'You *haggle* for us when you're back late'; fraught with difficulties. 'It's a *haggling* job'

haine *n.* an enclosure. 'Get those sheep back in the *haine*'

hairs *n.* the hair-cloths used in cider-making (*hairs* were laid alternately with layers of apples in a cider press)

hales *n.* plough handles

half-baptised *adj.* (also **half-named**) said of a child who has been baptised by the midwife, or privately (N HEREFS, MON BORDER)

half-saved *adj.* (also **half-strained**) simple, half-witted

halfoaf moulsin *n.* a stupid person, idiot (W HEREFS)

ham *n.* a flat meadow next to a river

hames *n.* (also **ames**; pl. **hameses, ameses**) the metal or wooden bars on a working horse's collar, to which the traces are fixed

han *v.* have. 'You *han* a good horse there'

handler *n.* the sideman or second to a boxer, pugilist etc.

handstaff *n.* the handle of a *flail*

handy *adv.* nearly, almost. 'The nearest shop is *handy* a mile from here'

hanger *n.* the gate post on which a gate is hung

hangstree *n.* (also **hangstry**) the upright part of a gate itself, to which the hinges are attached (N HEREFS)

hank *v., n.* hold. '*Hank* on tight and don't let go!'

hanky-panky *n.* cunning dealing

hanna *v.* (also **havena**) has not or have not (NW HEREFS)

Hanover *n.* 'Well, I'll go to *Hanover*!' is an expression of astonishment akin to 'Well, I'll be damned!' A local variation of this is: 'Well, I'll go to Hay!'

hansel *n.* (also **handsel**) the first money received for a sale on a given day (which may then be spat on for luck)

hantle *n.* a lot. 'A *hantle* of money' (N HEREFS)

hard nap *n.* a shrewd, clever person. 'She's a *hard nap*'

hardheads *n.* (also **hard-heads**) a name used for several 'weeds', including plantains and knapweed. Also sometimes used for red burnet (KENTCHURCH)

harkener *n.* an eavesdropper, listener

harp *n.* (also **arp**) a scythe

harried *v.* to be physically obstructed or frustrated

harried up *adj.* frustrated, anxious

harriff *n.* (also **herriff, ayriff**) goosegrass or cleevers (plant)

haslet *n.* (also **aslet**) a type of sausage made of pig entrails

hasper *v.* (also **hesper**) to hasten, hurry. 'You'll have to *hasper* to get there in time' (N HEREFS)

haul-in *n.* relating to the harvest, a good *haul-in* generally means a harvest well gathered, or with a good yield

haulm *n.* that part of e.g. potatoes, peas, beans etc. that is above ground

haut *v., n.* hold. 'Get a tight *haut* on those reins'

hauve *n.* the handle of an axe

haux *v., n.* stroll. 'I'll *haux* over to yours later'

haw! waggoner's instruction to a horse to turn left (NE HEREFS). See Waggoners' calls, p. 178

hayfer *n.* (also **ayfer**) a heifer

haytick *n.* whinchat (bird)

hazumjazum *adj.* straightforward, just so. 'Everything's *hazumjazum*' = everything is all right; nothing is amiss

head stall *n.* a stout bridle for fastening a horse to a manger

headaches *n.* poppies (their scent was believed to bring on headaches)

heal *v.* to cover over seed sown by a harrow, for example

heart *adj.* (also **in good heart**) of crops and land: fertile, doing well. 'My spuds are in *good heart*'

heartful *adj.* (also **heartwhole, heartwell**) well in terms of appetite, in good spirits. 'I was *heartful* when he told me'

heaver *n.* a gate that has to be lifted, not pushed, in order to open it (GOLDEN VALLEY). 'Close that *heaver* after you'

heavle *n.* a fork (particularly a three-pronged dung-fork)

hedgepig *n.* hedgehog (a gypsy word)

hedgerman *n.* (also **hedger**) a man who dresses hedges

hedge'uck *n.* (also **hedgebill**) hedge hook, slash hook (stronger than a *brush hook*)

heft *v.*, *n.* 1. to feel or judge something by lifting it. 'This wool *hefts* well'; to raise or heave; 2. to do something in a leisurely fashion. 'She did it at her own *heft*'; 3. a large number of something, usually birds or animals. 'There's a *heft* of starlings in that tree' (BRAMPTON BRYAN)

hell-rake *n.* a large, broad rake used in hay-making

helm *n.* a tine handle (N HEREFS)

herds *n.* the refuse of flax (linseed); also called *tow*

herence *adv.* (also **therence**) hence, thence

hermiting *v.* keeping to oneself. 'She's *hermiting* upstairs'

hern *n.*, *pron.* 1. heron; 2. hers

hersking *n.* a hearse (ROWLSTONE)

hespel *v.* (also **huspel**) 1. to worry, harass; 2. to run about. 'Don't *hespel* about it' (N HEREFS)

heyst! *v.* (also **heist, hice, hist, hoist, hysht, hyst**) hush! be still!

hickle *n.* (also **hickol**) green woodpecker

hidlock *n.* a state of concealment. 'He left last week and has been *hidlock* since'

higgler *n.* a pedlar

high in the breastbone *adj.* (also **high-breasted**) said of someone who puts on airs, proud, arrogant (*high in the breastbone* used in LEOMINSTER; *high-breasted* in ROSS)

hile *v.* 1. of cattle: to butt or strike with the head or horns; to toss the head; 2. the swinging part of a flail

hiling *v.* tearing. 'The cows have been *hiling* at the hedge'

hilt *n.* a gilt; a young female pig, a sow kept for breeding, which has yet to have any young

hindersome *adj.* hindering, particularly of the weather. 'This *hindersome* rain has stopped us getting the hay in'

hirple *v.* to limp, hobble. 'He's been *hirpling* since his fall'

hisht *v.* listen. '*Hisht* you kids!'

hisn *pron.* his. 'That's *hisn* land'

hit *n.* a plentiful crop of fruit. 'We had a great *hit* of apples'

ho! ho! ho! call or cry used to drive cattle. See Calls to animals, p. 177

hob *n.* the third swarm of bees. See *cast*

hobbing *v.* hollering, whooping, making a loud noise (LLANWARNE)

hobbledy-hoy *n.* neither man nor boy; a youngster

hoblionker *n.* a child's name for a conker. See *oblionker*

hobs *n.* 'They go like the *hobs* of hell' = they go like fury; like the devil

hocks *v.* to cut (e.g. wood) in an un-workmanlike or inexpert fashion. 'He's *hocksed* that brush all uneven'

hog *v.* to *hog* a hedge is to trim it closely

hognel *adj.* (also **ognel**) 1. surly, disagreeable, stubborn (W HEREFS); 2. awkward, uneven; 3. ignorant; rude

hogwelly *adj.* large, hoggish. 'A great *hogwelly* fellow'

hoi! hoi! hoi! call or cry used to drive sheep. See Calls to animals, p. 177

hoil *v.* restless cattle using their horns on each other are said to be *hoiling* one another

hoisht! hush! '*Hoisht* your prattling!'

holdover *n.* 1. 'the Herefordshire custom in a Candlemas (2 Feb) tenancy whereby the outgoing tenant could retain the house, a part of the buildings and the *boosey pasture* until 1 May, to enable him to consume all of his produce before quitting the property' (WL)

hollop *v.* to scoop out the inside of an apple, turnip etc.

holme screech *n.* mistle thrush

holt *v.* to take hold of, to grip. 'Go and get a *holt* of them'

holtless *adj.* (also **holdless**) careless, heedless

hom *n.* (also **homme, holme**) 1. home; 2. a low, flat place near a river. Used in field-names as a descriptive ('*Homme* Banks', 'Woodcock's *Homme*' etc.). As a place-name generally, it is common around Ledbury and Ross

homber *n.* (also **hommer**) hammer

homes *n.* (also **hames**) the metal parts surrounding a collar to which the traces are attached

hommoxing *v.* messing about with food. 'Stop *hommoxing* with it, and get it down you'

hone *v.*, *adj.* 1. to thrash, beat (BREDWARDINE); 2. lazy

honesty *n.* old man's beard, traveller's joy (plant)

hongered *adj.* hungry. 'I wasn't half *hongered*'

hooch *v.* (also **hootch**) to sit in a heap, to crouch

hood *n.* (also **'ood**) wood

hoof *n.* bullfinch (N HEREFS)

hook *n.* (also **huck, 'uck**) a long-handled implement for trimming hedges. See *badging-*, *bagging-*, *fagging-*, *repping-* and *wid-hook*

hook-fingered *adj.* prone to thieving; acquisitive

hookin' *n.* a quantity. 'A fair *hookin'* = a good amount

hoolet *n.* owl

hoolety *adj.* (also **hooleting**) like an owl. 'A moping *hoolety* creature'

hoont *n.*, *adj.* (also **woont**) a mole. The word appears in the phrase: 'As slick as a *hoont*' (typically applied e.g. to a well-groomed horse)

hoop *n.* (also **cock hoop**) bullfinch (from its call). The word appears in a Ledbury church register of 1711 (LEDBURY)

hoop! hoop! call for driving loose cattle. See Calls to animals, p. 177

hoosk *n.* a dry cough

hoosuck *n.* (also **hussock, tussock**) 1. the husk, a disease of cattle; 2. sometimes applied to a hacking or hard, dry cough which is the most obvious symptom of husk, or generally to hard, dry coughs

hoot! to a horse, an instruction to turn right. See Waggoners' calls, p. 178

hop dog *n.* a white-striped grub which feeds on the hop leaf. Less commonly called 'ladies' lap dog'

hop kiln *n.* a purpose-built building for drying hops

hop-abouts *n.* apple dumplings

hop-bagger *n.* a press, powered or turned by hand, used to compress hops into a *hop-pocket*

hop-bines *n.* the long, climbing stems of the hop plant

hop-hook *n.* a type of hook (sickle) used in cutting hops

hop-picker *n.* (also **hop-picking morning, hop-picking weather**) a term used to describe fine weather in late August and September, characterised by early mists and heavy dews, with sun and sharp air. 'It's a *hop-picker* this morning!' (BISHOPS FROME)

hop-pocket *n.* a sack *c.*6-ft long into which hops are pressed by a *hop-bagger* after drying in a *hop kiln*. The compressed hops are stored and sold in this form, with a *hop-pocket* typically weighing around 80 kg

hope *v., n.* 1. to help. 'I *hoped* them stack the hay bales'; 2. a small valley branching out into a larger one (used in place-names: e.g. Sollers *hope*, Wool*hope*, Fown*hope* etc.)

hopple *v.* to hobble an animal (i.e. tie its legs to prevent it from wandering; especially horses etc.)

hopples *n.* apples

hoppowles *n.* hop poles; the upright timbers in a *hopyard* carrying the supporting wirework for growing hops

hopyard *n.* (also **hop-yard**) a field in which hops are grown

horn cag *n.* (also **arn cag**) used in the phrase 'As tough as an old *horn cag*' (i.e. very tough, hard). *Cag* derives from 'keg' (STAUNTON-ON-WYE)

horse hoe *n.* a horse-drawn cultivator, first recorded in use in the 1830s

horse-block *n.* a mounting block

horse-lopin' *v.* horse dealing (e.g. at a horse fair)

horsestinger *n.* hornet (MUCH DEWCHURCH)
hoshy *adj.* cider may be described as *hoshy* when it has lost its sugars and sometimes has the flavour of a steel knife
houselling-cloth *n.* a white cloth draped over the altar-rail during the celebration of Holy Communion (an old custom once observed in some parish churches)
housen *n.* houses (ROSS)
hoven *n.* a windy distension of the belly in cattle
howgy *adj.* (also **howgeous**) enormous, huge
howlet *n.* (also **hullet**) 1. a stupid person, a fool; 2. an owlet
hows *n.* technique. Said of a man working hard but making a poor job of it. 'He don't seem to have no *hows*'
huck *n.* (also **'uck**) cutting hook. See *brummock* and *wid'uck*
hucking *n.* (also **'ucking**) 1. a shift (farm work); 2. a load
hud *n.* husk or shell
hudjuck *n.* a mess, a state of disarray. 'The house is in such a *hudjuck*' (NW HEREFS)
huffcap *n.* 1. a type of perry-pear; 2. the resultant perry (MUCH MARCLE)
humbuz *n.* a cockchafer (beetle)
humby *n.* nonsense (from 'humbug') (WIGMORE)
humersome *adj.* full of whims or fancies. 'She was ever a *humersome* dreamer'
hummocks n. feet. 'Get your filthy *hummocks* off my clean table!' (ROSS)
hump *v.* to carry (particularly an awkward load)
hunch *n.* a lump or chunk. 'Pass me a *hunch* of cheese'
hunkering *v.* crowding, generally applied to cattle (STAUNTON-ON-WYE)

hurd *v.* (also **herd**) to store or hoard

hurden *adj.* (also **herden, herdenan, hurdon**) made from hards or herds (a coarse fabric); or sacking or an old sack. 'A *hurden* coat'

hurry *n.* time, occasion. 'We can't stay this *hurry*'

hurrysome *adj.* very hasty. 'Don't be so *hurrysome*'

hurtle *n.* a spot (possibly deriving from heraldry: *hurt* or *heurte* is a blue spot in heraldry)

hutch *n.* a chest or coffer (a church chest)

hwyl *n.* a frenzy, rapture (GOLDEN VALLEY)

hyle *v.* to reject or throw out (LINGEN)

I

if so be if that is so. 'That's all well then, *if so be*'

iffing and offing (also **ivering, ivving, overing, ovvering**) dithering, wavering in mind, being indecisive. 'Pick one and stop this *iffing and offing*' (E HEREFS)

ignorant *adj.* lacking in manners (S HEREFS)

ile *v.* (also **hile**) to attack with horns (of a bull or cow etc.) 'He looks like he'd *ile* me if I stepped in his field'

iles *n.* (also **spiles**) awns (the hairs or bristles) of barley, wheat etc.

ill-blended *adj.* (also **ill-blained, ill-relished, ill-sorted**) irritable, disagreeable. 'He's an *ill-blended* old bugger' (BRAMPTON BRYAN)

ill-convenient *adj.* inconvenient

ill-wish *v.* to cast a spell, bewitch

imp *n., v.* a bud or a young shoot of coppice that has been cut; to *imp* is to bud. 'The roses are *imping* nicely'

imperence *n.* (also **imference**) impertinence, rudeness, sauciness (N HEREFS)

improve on *v.* to approve of (ARCHENFIELD)

in course of course. '*In course* you can have a drink'

in some form *adv.* very considerably; impressively. 'He could drink cider *in some form*'

incense *v.* (also **insense, insense**) to inform, instruct, make to understand, explain. 'I have *incensed* him of your offer' (AYLTON, N HEREFS)

inchable *adv.* (also **inchmeal, inchmull**) 1. inch-by-inch, thoroughly. 'I searched for it *inchable*' (ARCHENFIELD); 2. little by little, gradually

ind *n.* inn. Another instance of the termination 'd' found in Herefordshire dialect, frequently found after the letter 'n' (e.g. 'A bottle of *wind*'; 'Rose and *Crownd*' etc.)

inna *v.* isn't, is not. 'She *inna* dressed yet' (N HEREFS)

innocent *n.* 1. a person of weak intellect; 2. a small child

inoffensive *adj.* innocent, pure-minded (N HEREFS)

inons *n.* onions. 'A rope of *inons*'

interceding *adj.* an *interceding* man is one who is ready to take the lead; a prominent person

into *prep.* short of. 'He lives just *into* a mile away'

inwards *n.* the entrails of an animal (corruption of *innards*)

iss *adv., n.* yes. 'I'd say *iss* to another beer'

Isaac *n.* 1. a scythe (so-called after the popular and well regarded scythe-maker, Isaac Nash); 2. a hedge sparrow. See *blue Isaac*

ivvy *n.* ivy

izzard *n.* the letter 'z'. 'Zebra starts with an *izzard*'

J

jack-in-the-green *n.* (also **jack-in-the-pulpit**) wild arum

jack-in-the-hedge *n.* the name given to a number of wayside plants (most commonly to garlic mustard)

jack squealer *n.* swift (bird) (LEDBURY)

jack stones *n.* pebbles or rounded stones, 'several times larger than one's feet' (WL), sometimes found in local clay (HEREFS, MON BORDER)

jacky-five-stones *n.* a children's game similar to 'knuckle bones', played with five small, round pebbles

jackystone *n.* any small, round pebble, but specifically one used in the game *jacky-five-stones*

jag *n.* 1. a small load; not a full load ('a *jag* of hay'); 2. a bit ('a tidy *jag*' = a good bit)

jagging *v.* carting hay. 'I'll be *jagging* during the harvest'

jammock *v.* (also **jammuck**) to crush, squeeze, press tightly

jangle *v.*, *n.* 1. to prattle, chatter; 2. to wrangle, quarrel; 3. a tangle. 'Your wool's got into a *jangle*' (SW HEREFS)

jannock *adj.* (also **jonnock**) 1. fair, honest, straightforward (LINGEN); 2. pleasant, agreeable (said of a man when he works pleasantly: 'he's a *jonnuck* sort'); 3. hospitable; one who pays his fair share for drinks (LEOMINSTER)

jasper *n.* wasp (from the old French word *guespe* or modern French *guêpe*, meaning 'wasp')

jaunders *n.* jaundice

jawl *v.* to knock someone. 'He *jawled* me against the wall'

jelly hooter *n.* owl. A phrase inspired by the tremulous call usually heard at night

jet *n.* a descent, decline or declivity. 'It rolled down the *jet*'

jewel *v.* to put a ring in a pig's nose. Ringing the noses of pigs is sometimes called 'marrying the pigs'

jigging *v.* traipsing, trudging; going on foot

job *v.* to jab. 'She gave me a sharp *job* in the ribs'

joey *n.* a silver threepenny piece. 'Lend us a *joey*' (WIGMORE)

joggle *v.*, *n.* to shake. 'Give him a *joggle* to wake him up'

johnny *n.* a silly fellow

jolly *adj.* fat

jorum *n.* 1. a large helping of food or drink (N HEREFS); 2. a large jug or ewer

joucet *adj.* unwell. See *middling*

joy *n.* jay (bird) (ROSS)

jubbin *n.* donkey

jubilous *adj.* (also *djubilous*) 1. jubilant, very glad or happy; 2. sometimes appears as a corruption of 'dubious'

just *adv.* 'I got here but *just*' = I arrived only this minute

just now *adv.* soon, presently. 'I'll go and see those cows *just now*' (MON BORDER)

justicing *v.* going before magistrates. 'Do that again and you'll be *justicing*'

justly *adv.* exactly, precisely. 'I'll be here at *justly* midday'

K

kag *n.* (also **kyag**) a broken-off bough. See *stoggle*

kay'old *n.* keyhole

keagh *v.* (also **keer**) used in calling to dogs and people (probably an abbreviation of 'look here')

keck *v.* (also **keek**) to retch or vomit; to clear one's throat (onomatopoeic) (MON BORDER)

keckfisted *adj.* (also **keggie-fisted**) ham-fisted, clumsy. 'The *keckfisted* fool dropped and smashed it'

kecks *n.* (also **kecksies, kex**) cow-parsley, hemlock or similar types of hollow-stemmed plants (umbelifers)

kecky *adj.* poorly. 'She was feeling *kecky*'

kedlock *n.* charlock (plant)

keech *n.*, *v.* 1. a clot (N HEREFS); 2. a lump of cake or fat as might be sold to a tallow-chandler (candle maker); 3. to make into cake as wax or tallow; 4. a slab of material such as well-settled hay as cut from a rick, or well-trodden manure that can be separated into layers. Analogous to what is understood by the word 'wodge'

keen *v.* to sharpen. 'Go and *keen* that blade for me'

keep *n.* 1. pasture; 2. 'To *keep* market' = to attend market for the purpose of selling

keffel *n.* (also **kefful**) a disparaging term for a horse or person, from the Welsh *ceffyl* = horse (BRAMPTON BRYAN)

kelp *n.*, *v.* (also **kyowp**) 1. the bark of a fox; 2. the yelp of a dog; 3. to scold or nag. 'He's been *kelping* me to do it'

kelute *n.* a shindy; a disturbance or quarrel. 'A noisy *kelute*'

kelvie *n.* miscellaneous goods of little value; oddments. 'What a load of *kelvie*' (PEMBRIDGE)

kep *v.* kept. 'She always *kep* a tidy house'

kerf *n.*, *v.* (pronounced 'kearf') (also **kerf, kierf, kurf, kyerf, kyurf**) 1. a tool, typically home-made from a worn spade bent almost at right-angles at the *langet* and fitted to a long shaft. Used for earthing up potatoes, hops etc.; 'To *kerf* up spuds' = to dig up potatoes using a *kerf*; 2. a lump of hay cut from a rick with a hay-knife

kernel *n.* a seedling apple or pear

kerp! kerp! (also **kepp! kepp!**) call to poultry. See Calls to animals, p. 177

ketch holt *v.* to catch hold. '*Ketch holt* of them reins'

kettle-broth *n.* poor man's bread and milk (consisting of bread soaked in hot water with the addition of pepper, salt and a nut of butter)

kevin *n.* (also **caving, cavend, caving**) a part of the round of beef (from the Welsh *cefn* = ridge or back)

kibble *n.* a piece or pieces of wood

kick *v.* to sting (as a wasp, bee etc.)

kickle *adj.* (also **keckle**) flighty; weak in the stomach

kid *n.* faggot of wood (N HEREFS)

kiddle *n.*, *v.* to dribble, as children

kierlock *n.* charlock (plant) (ROSS)

kill *n.* a kiln, as hop-*kill*, brick-*kill*, lime-*kill* (the 'n' is not pronounced)

kill-howling *v.*, *n.* a hop-drier, on duty continuously night and day, sleeps on the spot for an hour or two at times when his duties permit. At night, this is a lonely job. On occasions he would invite one or two friends to keep him company overnight, when much cider was drunk. This visiting is known as *kill-howling* (*kill* from 'kiln')

kilt *v.* killed

kimist *adj.* (the 'ki' pronounced as per 'my') (also **kimit, kymist, kyment, kymet**) 1. foolish, half-witted, daft (W HEREFS); 2. befuddled, intoxicated, drunk (WIGMORE)

kinchin *n.* a little child (from the German *kindlein* or *kindchen*) (W HEREFS)

kind *adj.* 1. of crops, animals, people, health, weather: good, favourable, flourishing; 2. well-placed, effective (STAUNTON-ON-WYE, ROWLSTONE)

kindly *adj.* prosperous

kinowing *v.* making up. 'She's been *kinowing* the fire'

kipe *n.* a circular basket holding two or three *pecks*

kippin' crows *v.* driving or keeping off rooks and crows

kiss-me-at-the-garden-gate *n.* (also **kiss-me-quick**) 1. sweet woodruff; 2. pansy

kitty-brandtail *n.* (also **katie-brandtail**) redstart (bird)

kitty-whitethroat *n.* whitethroat (bird)

kivest *n.* collared dove or wood pigeon (BREDWARDINE). See *quist*

knap *n.* a stretch of road ascending steeply; a *pitch*

knile *n.* (also **nile, ile**) the shorter, striking part of a flail

knit up *adj.* 1. drawn up, stiffened with rheumatism or cramp; 2. 'The birds are all *knit up*' = their feathers are all fluffed up with cold (LEDBURY)

knobble *v.* to hammer or hit feebly. 'Stop *knobbling* it and give it a proper whack!'

knot *n.* 1. flower-*knot* = flower bed (thus *knot* garden); 2. to be in a *knot* about something is to not know what to do; to be in a muddle (MON BORDER)

know to *v.* to know of; to know about. 'I *know to* him'

knowed *v.* knew (past tense of the verb 'to know'). 'I *knowed* him when he were a lad'

knurdy *adj.* 1. unthrifty. 'He's *knurdy* and spends when he should save'; 2. a litter of pigs looking unfit and neglected might be referred to as a '*knurdy* looking lot'

koop! koop! call to horses. See Calls to animals, p. 177

koy-yer *n.* choir

kucky *adj.* dirty, messy (of children or animals). 'Get cleaned up, you *kucky* bunch!' (GOLDEN VALLEY)

kutch *v.* (also **kutch down**) to squat

kyagging *v.* ripping or tearing

kyander *v.* look yonder!

kyind *adj.* (also **kind**) well; good. 1. referring to health: 'I'm not feeling *kyind*'; 2. referring to the weather: 'It's not looking *kyind* out there'; 3. referring to soil and crops: 'The spuds are looking *kyind*'

kype *n.* (also **kipe, kupe, kuype**) a large, oval container made of cleft wood strips, used for carrying food (such as chopped mangolds or chaff to cattle); a large, coarsely-made basket. See *whisket*

L

lace *v.* to thrash or beat. 'I'll *lace* your hide!'

lade *v.* to bail, to ladle

ladies' lap dog *n.* see *hop dog*

ladies' parasols *n.* star of Bethlehem (flower)

lady cow *n.* ladybird

lady's purse *n.* slipper flower, lady's purse

lady's smock *n.* cuckoo flower, lady's smock

lady's thimble *n.* harebell (flower)

lagger *n.* a broad, green lane, little or not used as a road. 'He lives in a cottage at the end of the *lagger*'

laid by *v.* laid up, incapacitated. 'I was *laid by* after the fall'

lambs' tails *n.* hazel or willow catkins

lamentable *adv.* extremely, very. 'I'm *lamentable* hungry'

lammockin *v.* (pronounced 'lommockin') slouching. 'Stop *lammockin* and sit up straight'

land *n.* that part of ploughing between *reans* formed by an equal number of furrows falling in opposite directions, the two central furrows forming the *top*

landshut *n.* a flood of water over land (W HEREFS)

landtree *n.* (also **lantree**) the bar on a plough or harrow, to which the traces are attached (N & W HEREFS)

langet *n.* (also **langett, languet**) 1. the tongue of a buckle or a spade; 2. the projections on the hilt of a sword that lie outside the scabbard; 3. the straps on the heads of some hammers, holding them to the shaft; 4. a long, narrow strip of land (from the French *languette* = tongue)

lantle *n.* a piece or loaf. 'Pass us a *lantle* of bread'

lap *v.* to wrap up; envelop

lap-raskels *n.* old coats or rugs, and suchlike

lap up *v.* to wrap up. '*Lap up* those apples in brown paper'

lapesing *v.* traipsing

lapesy *adj.* sticky, dirty

larn *v.* 1. to teach; 2. to learn

larpin *n.* a small boy (BRAMPTON BRYAN)

larrup *v., n.* 1. to thrash, chastise; 2. hobbledehoy, stripling, awkward youth (BRAMPTON BRYAN)

larruping *n.* a beating. 'He deserves a good *larruping*'

lattage *n.* a speech impediment (ARCHENFIELD)

laughing bessie *n.* green woodpecker

lawter *n.* of eggs: a clutch; the number of eggs laid by a chicken or duck etc. (W HEREFS)

lawyer *n.* a bramble or other thorny stem caught in one's clothes; a long land briar (DILWYN)

lay *v.* of crops: to flatten. 'The corn's been *laid* by the wind'

lay-abed *n.* a lazy person

laylock *n.* lilac (plant)

lazy wind *n.* a wind that blows straight through one (i.e. a wind that is too lazy to go round) (MUCH MARCLE)

leads *n.* (pronounced 'leds') 'large leaden pans on four legs that hold milk for creaming' (WL)

leafing *v.* pulling off the leafy remnants left on hop wires in early summer, prior to the new growth

leaping block *n.* mounting block (for getting onto a horse)

lear *n., adj.* (also **leer**) 1. the hollow under the ribs; 2. empty. 'I feel *lear* in my stomach'; 3. when a horse is sold at a horse fair without a halter, the horse is sold *lear* (horses generally being sold with a new halter at a horse fair); a horse that is harnessed but drawing nothing is known as a '*lear* horse'

leasing *v.* gleaning, gathering. 'He's *leasing* the hay'

leasow *n.* pasture land. Often used as part of a field-name (e.g. Ox *Leasow*, Parson's *Leasow* etc.)

leathering bat *n.* pipistrelle bat

leeze *n.* (also **lease, leaze**) to glean

leisure *v.* to cause to be idle. 'The tractor's puncture *leisured* me awhile' (KINGSLAND)

lennow *adj.* (also **linnow**) 1. flexible, workable; 2. active; 3. limp (as dead or unconscious) (LEOMINSTER, N HEREFS)

lepping-stone *n.* (also **leppin' stone**) a mounting block (S HEREFS)

leuth *n.* warmth, as lost from a garment when it wears thin

lew-warm *adj.* luke-warm, tepid

lezzar *n.* a meadow; *leasow*

liars *n.* lawyers

lie-a-side *n.* (also **lie-by, lie-a-like**) a mistress, as distinct from a wife (S HEREFS BORDER)

lief *adv., v.* (pronounced 'lif') (also **liefer, liever, lif, liffer**) willingly, preferably; to prefer. 'I'd as *lief* stay in bed'

lift *n.* a joint of beef. 'That's a lovely bit of *lift*'

ligger *n.* a stitch or thread

lighted *v.* to be *lighted* is to be delivered of a child

lighten *v.* 1. to cheer up; 2. to shake up hay or grain

like *adv., conj.* 1. often used at the end of a sentence in a diminutive sense ('It's getting cold, *like*'); 2. more *like* = better ('Now that's more *like*!'); 3. as *like* as not = probably ('I'll go to the pub as *like* as not')

limbers *n.* cart-shafts

lion *n.* dandelion. 'Pick me a bunch of *lions*' (MON BORDER)

lip *n.* (also **lip-talk**) impudence, sassiness

lissen *n.* (also **lizzen**) a cleft in a rock

lissom *adj.* (also **litsome**) lithe and active; bright or cheerful (ROWLSTONE)

liverdy *adj.* soil of unbroken consistency

lixom *adj.* (also **licksome**) amiable. 'He's a *lixom* fellow'

loaves *n.* simpletons, half-witted folk. From the saying 'In with the *loaves*, out with the cakes': in old bread ovens the loaves were placed at the back and the cakes that cooked more quickly in the front, so that they could be taken out first. The inference of *loaves* is of being 'half-baked'

lock *n.* 1. a puddle of water; 2. '*lock* of wool' and '*lock* of hay' are used in same way as '*lock* of hair'

logger *n.* a wedding ring (UPTON BISHOP)

loggy *adj.* thickset, generally applied to cattle. 'That's a *loggy* bunch of Herefords'

lollop *n.* (also **dollop**) a generous portion (N HEREFS). 'He's a growing lad so give him a good *lollop* of stew'

lomber *v.* to move heavily or clumsily; to lumber about

lombering *adj.* awkward, ungainly

lommaking *v., adj.* 1. love-making; 2. idling, clumsy (ARCHENFIELD)

lompering *v., adj.* idling

lonck *n.* 1. the groin; 2. a stage or resting place for vehicles on a public road (BREDWARDINE)

long acre *n.* (also **long meadow**) the grass verge along a roadside. The old phrase, 'He grazes his *ship* [sheep] on the *long acre*' was a way of saying that someone was mean

long company *n.* gypsies (BRAMPTON BRYAN)

long gears *n.* horse gear (specifically the collar and *hames*, backband and traces with *spreader*)

long 'ooking *n.* (also **long 'ucking**) a long bout of work (especially of ploughing) (BRAMPTON BRYAN)

longtail *n.* pheasant (WIGMORE)

long-winded *adj.* slow, but not restricted to speech. 'She was *long-winded* in paying her bill'

lonk *n.* 1. the hip joint; 2. a depression in the road surface (ROSS); 3. a dingle that is not steep-sided. See *lonck*

lont *n.* low-lying land

loo *adj.* (also **loo warm**) luke warm

look *v.* (also **to look to**) to look round and see that all is in order. 'Will you *look* the cattle for me tomorrow?'
look slippy! *v.* be quick! (SUTTON ST NICHOLAS)
look up! *v.* look out!
looth *n.* (also **leuth, lewth**) warmth
lop and top *n., v.* the top branches of a felled tree; to cut the top branches of a tree (MON BORDER)
lost *adj.* famished, starving. 'I'm *lost* for want of me grub'
lot *v.* resolve, settle. 'I *lotted* to leave'
louse *v.* enliven (often spoken of ale: '*louse* it up')
low *n.* a mound, tump, as in the name Worme*low* etc.
low Sunday *n.* the next Sunday following Easter
lowk *n.* a heavy blow (W HEREFS)
lown *n.* a hen that is a poor layer (BRAMPTON BRYAN)
luffer *n.* a louvre (a slatted opening to let in air)
lug *n.* 1. a given quantity of wood; 2. a pole
lugging hay *v.* carting hay (N HEREFS)
lugtit *n.* a strong-sucking calf (W HEREFS)
Lukestet *n.* literally 'Luke's tide': the season of St Luke's Day, 18 October (N HEREFS). There was a *Lukestet* Fair at Bridgnorth in Shropshire
lumbersome *adj.* (also **lombersome**) heavy, awkward to move; cumbersome
lumper *n.* a child or animal growing out of infancy, filling out and becoming sturdy (STAUNTON-ON-WYE)
lunch *n.* lump
lunches *n., adj.* (also **lunchy**) wet, heavy soil digs '*lunchy*' or 'comes up in *lunches*', i.e. does not break and holds the mark of the spade; stiff and in hard clods (ROSS)

lunge *v.* 1. to train and tame a horse with a long rein; 2. to ill-treat an animal by throwing stones or beating with a stick (N HEREFS)

lungeous *adj.* 1. cruel (especially to animals); 2. vindictive, unmanageable (N HEREFS); 3. quarrelsome; 4. awkward, clumsy (ROSS); 5. energetic, quick moving

lurcher *n.* a potato left in the ground when the crop has been lifted

lush *v.* to beat down with boughs (e.g. a wasps nest)

luthorn *n.* lucerne (plant)

luxrous *adj.* luxurious

lye *n.* water in which wood ashes have been steeped (this produces a solution that can be used e.g. for making soap)

lynen *n.* a large bundle of straw from the threshing floor (KENTCHURCH)

M

mad meg *n.* (also **madnep, mednip**) the root of white bryony, which is toxic and sometimes eaten by cattle

madge *n.* magpie

maffering *v.* literally 'May-Fairing'. 'He's gone *maffering*' = he's gone to the May Fair; or, more loosely, he's gone out to enjoy himself

mag *v.* to scold

magget *n.* (also **maggoty pie**) a magpie

maggotty *adj.* (also **maggoty**) 1. said of a cross, fretful child; 2. frisky, playful

maiden's honesty *n.* wild clematis or old man's beard (*honesty* here bears the sense of chastity)

mainish *adv.* particularly, very, but not extremely. 'The job is a *mainish* tricky one' = the job is a difficult one (albeit not impossible)

maister *n.* master

maister teddy *n.* badger

make love to the cook *v.* when a ploughman's plough-wheel squeals for lack of lubrication, he is told to go and '*make love to the cook*' (i.e. to beg some grease from the kitchen)

make the door *v.* to make fast the door; to shut and bolt it

malkin *n.* (pronounced 'maawkin') (also **maukin, mawk, mawkin**) 1. scarecrow (*mawk*: GOLDEN VALLEY); 2. slattern

mammocks *n., v.* (pronounced 'mommocks') fragments, scraps; 2. to maul or mangle

market peart *adj.* (also **market peert, market p'yert**) a bit tipsy or lively after a few drinks on market day

marls *n.* (also **marvels**) marbles

marnin! good morning!

marple *n.* (also **mauple**) maple tree (S HEREFS)

mashes *n.* the threads of a screw (KENTCHURCH)

masterful *adj.* unmanageable. 'She was a *masterful* tyke'

mat *n.* to stir up the earth around potatoes (KENTCHURCH)

math *n.* a day's work for a mower, approximating to an acre

mather *n.* (the first syllable pronounced as 'lathe') ox-eye daisy, viewed as a farmland weed (plural *matheren*)

mathon *n.* (also **maython**) wild camomile

mattock *n.* large hoe, kerf or stocker

mauk *v.* to mimic

maumble *v.* to mess about while doing anything

maunch *n.* all to bits. 'Smashed to *maunch*' (ARCHENFIELD)

maunder *v.* to speak incoherently, as a person in a feverish state, or while asleep or drunk. 'Hark at him *maunder*'

Mavis *n.* song thrush

mawn *n.* peat, turf (a *mawn*-pit is a peat-pit)

May blobs *n.* kingcups, marsh marigold (plant)

maybush *n.* hawthorn (MON BORDER)

maythering *v.* babbling like an imbecile (BREDWARDINE)

mazzard *n.* a head or face

meal *adj.*, *n.* 1. implying division: in addition to piece*meal*, a carcass might be jointed limb*meal*; an intermittent pain might come on fit*meal* etc.; 2. the quantity of milk yielded by a cow during milking

meare *n.* (also **mere**) an uncultivated strip of land

meat *v.*, *n.* 1. to feed animals. 'I'm off to *meat* the cows'; 2. feed or fodder for horses and cattle

meaty things *n.* cattle, sheep (*meaty* = fleshy but not yet fat)

medicine *n.* drink; alcohol. 'He likes a spot of *medicine*'

meeuxing *v.* messing anything about in the mouth. 'Stop *meeuxing* your food, and swallow it!'

menagery *n.* a contrivance (N HEREFS)

mend your draft *v.* finish your drink and have another one (related to *swipe your horn*)

ment *adj.* mended. 'He *ment* the gate' (BISHOPS FROME)

mere *n.* the grass division between strips in an open field

mergal *n.* (also **mergle**) confusion or mess. A field of wheat flattened by heavy rain might be said to be 'in a *mergal*'

merkin *n.* a wig

merle *n.* blackbird

mess *n.* a term of contempt for anything small or weak

mewed *adj.* cooped up

mex out *v.* to clean out (a cow house or stable) (EARDISLAND)

middling *adj.* (also **middlin**) 1. in general terms, ill or unwell, in reply to 'How are you?' The meaning can vary depending on context and tone of voice. Thus, if someone is a little out of sorts, they might be *middling* or *a bit middling*; but if seriously ill they might be *pretty* or *very middling*. If the reply '*middling*' is uttered brightly, this would indicate the speaker is quite well; but if uttered dully, this would suggest he/ she is not well. See *joucet*. 'Diminutives [words used to create the meaning of smallness] are at all times used by the poor; but in a greater degree when they are conversing with superiors. The habit appears to have arisen from a desire to excite compassion, by making themselves appear ill off. They talk in the following way. If you ask "What sort of crop of potatoes have you?" "I think I shall have some taters." They would say no more if they expected the best possible crop. "How are you?" "*Middling*, or indifferent, well," would be the answer; though the person was not ill, and had not been ailing for years.' (GCL) 2. *middling* can also be applied to work that is not going well

miff *n.*, *v.* variant of tiff; sulk or huff; a falling out

milestone inspector *n.* a tramp (LEOMINSTER)

milkmaids *n.* lady's smock (plant) (FOWNHOPE)

mill-bill *n.* a tool for cutting grooves on a millstone

millard *n.* (also **millet**) a miller

mimmock *adj.*, *n.* (also **mimmockin, mimmocking**) 1. puny, feeble; 2. a weak or frail child

mimmocky *adj.* having little appetite; picking at one's food

mint *n.* a mite

minty *n.*, *adj.* 1. a pet name for, or mode of address to, a cat, used as 'puss' or 'pussy' might be; 2. full of mites ('*minty* cheese' is cheese with mites in it)

mirkshut *n.* twilight, the close of day and the final dwindling of its light by the gathering of dusk

miscall *v.* to say malicious or unkind things about someone

mishroom *n.* mushroom

mishterful *adj.* playful, mischievous

mishtiff *n.* (also **mistiff**) mischief

miskin *n.* (also **mixen**) manure heap, rubbish heap (LEOMINSTER, W HEREFS)

misler *n.* (also **mistletoe thrush**) mistle thrush

mislest *v.* molest

mistrust *v.* to doubt, but also (conversely) to expect or to fear: a confusion that arises due to the common use of the double negative: 'I *mistrust* he won't pay' = I doubt he'll pay; but 'I *mistrust* it'll rain later' = I expect it'll rain later

misword *n.* disagreement, misunderstanding; unkind word

mithered *adj.*, *v.* (also **moidered, moithered, mythered**) 1. bothered, confused, muddled; to *mither* = to muddle or perplex; *mithering* = confusing; 2. trembling, shaky in health (ROSS)

mitt *n.* (also **mit, butter mitt**) a wooden tub in which freshly-made butter is washed and salted

mix out *v.* clean out (WIGMORE). See *mex out*

mizzle *n.*, *v.* 1. light rain, drizzle; to drizzle; 2. to mislead, to give wrong information

mog *n.* (also **moggie, moggy**) pet name for a calf, or occasionally a young donkey (N HEREFS, GOLDEN VALLEY)
moil *v., n.* (also **mullock**) 1. to drudge, to work very hard; 2. sticky, wet mud or dirt (*mullock* used by Chaucer)
moiled *adj.* (also **mullocky**) 1. covered in dirt or wet mud (W HEREFS); 2. hornless: a sheep without horns is termed a *moiled* sheep
moithen *n.* field scabious (flower)
mollock *n.* (also **mullock**) dirt, litter, mess
momblement *n.* a state of confusion, disorder
mommet *n.* (also **mommel**) 1. a small figure. Originally a term of abuse, but also used with an element of pity or compassion: 'You poor little *mommet*'; 2. an effigy or scarecrow to frighten birds
mommock *n.* confusion
money in both pockets *n.* the plant honesty (*Lunaria*). So-called because the flat round seeds are visible through the transparent seed-case in which there are two lobes resembling pockets.
monkey *n.* (also **monkey pole**) long pole used for attaching the strings to the hooks on overhead wires in a *hopyard*
mooch *v.* (also **mouch**) to play truant for the purpose of blackberrying. 'His brother's off *mooching* again'
moocher *n.* one who skips school to go blackberrying; 2. a potato left in the ground, which comes up the following year. See *lurcher*
moolson *n.* donkey. An old word that had apparently become almost obsolete by the 1880s (BLACK MOUNTAINS)
mooly *adj.* hornless, referring to a cow (N HEREFS)

moonrakers *n.* Wiltshire men (derogatory)

moot *v.* 1. to dig up with a mattock; 2. said of e.g. pigs rooting or dogs scratching up the ground (KENTCHURCH)

mooter *v., n.* 1. to ridge ground; 2. a ridging plough that cuts a double furrow (N HEREFS)

mop *n.* a fair at which female farm servants were hired

mopple *v., adj.* said of an overgrown hedge. 'The hawthorn is all of a *mopple*'

morning wood *n.* kindling wood dried by the fireside overnight to light the fire in the morning

mort *n.* a large number, a great deal. 'A *mort* of trouble'

mortal *adv.* (also **mortally**) very, extremely, really. 'After eight pints he was *mortal* drunk' (ROSS)

morthen *n.* fireweed (rosebay willowherb) (KENTCHURCH), or possibly scabious (ORCOP)

mortify *v.* tease or annoy. 'Stop *mortifying* your sister'

mose *v.* to smoulder (*mosing* = burning without a flame)

mosey *adj.* (also **mosy**) gone soft, over-ripe, decayed, as apples, pears, turnips etc.

mosker *v.* to complain, grumble. 'Don't *mosker* so!'

mossel *n.* a morsel

moughten *n.* (pronounced 'mudgen') the mesentery (part of the intestine) of a pig, cooked on a long skewer

mote *n.* moth (SUTTON ST NICHOLAS)

mought *v.* might. 'It *mought* be true' (E HEREFS)

moughten *v.* might not. 'It *moughten* be true' (E HEREFS)

moup *v.* ('ou' pronounced as in 'cow') to mope (ROSS)

mouse *n.* 1. a pet name for a puppy; 2. a beef joint (WHITCHURCH)

mouse-ear *n.* forget-me-not (FOWNHOPE)

moust *adv.* (also **mowst**) almost. 'If I stand on tiptoe I can *moust* reach it'

mouster *v.* 1. to pulverise; 2. to moulder for compost

moutering *v.* taking no notice of, ignoring. 'I waved but he was *moutering* me'

mouzend *n.* (also **monzend, munzend**) the month's end after a death; the attendance of the relatives at church on the Sunday after a funeral (ROWLSTONE, WHITCHURCH). See *deathzear*

mow-burned *adj.* (also **mowburnt**) hay or corn carted when it is too damp and heated in the rick is *mow-burned*; more generally, hay or corn burnt by heating

mox *n.* a state of decay. 'The old farm's in such a sorry *mox*'

moyle *n.* a hornless cow or bull (ORCOP)

much *v.* to fondle, to make much of

mucher *n.* used negatively or in a derogatory way for a person or thing of little account; something that is not worth a great deal. 'He weren't much of a *mucher*'; 'That tool isn't a *mucher*'

muck-sweat *n., v.* heavy sweat (*muck-sweating* = sweating profusely)

mulkin *n.* 1. a scarecrow; 2. a simpleton (W HEREFS)

mullen *n.* (also **mullein**) a cart-horse bridle (E HEREFS)

mullock *n.* dirt, mud, slush, rubbish, litter

mullocks *n.* a slattern, a slovenly person

mumble-peg *n.* the peg holding the strings of an old-fashioned wooden mole-trap, which is tripped by the mole to operate the trap

mummiruffin *n.* (also **mumruffin, mum-ruffin, mummy-ruffin**) long-tailed tit

mummygob *v.* 1. to mumble; 2. to chew ineffectually. 'He's lost all his teeth and *mummygobs* his food'

munch *v.* to steal household provisions. 'She's been *munching* from the pantry again' (N HEREFS)

muncorn crop *n.* a mixture of different seeds sown to come up as one crop, for example rye and wheat for bread

muncorn team *n.* a mixed team of horses and oxen

munjer *v.* to mutter, to speak inarticulately

munna *v.* must not. 'You *munna* touch it while it's hot'

muntling *v.* wandering, straying. 'Don't you go *muntling* off now'

must *n.* (also **mush**) the residue of apples or pears after the extraction of juice in cider- or perry-making; ground apples or pears (also applicable to grapes and other fruit)

mye *v.* (also **mow**) to place grain in a rick

N

nail-passer *n.* (also **nail parster, nailpiercer, passer**) a gimlet (a hand-tool for boring holes in wood)

naked ladies *n.* autumn crocus

nan *n.* an interjection, signifying that the speaker does not hear or understand what has been said to him

nanny *n.* a small, three-wheeled cart or *dobbin*

narra *pron.* (also **nerrun**) not any; not one. 'I seen *narra*' (N HEREFS). *Nerrun* probably derives from 'never a one'. Often used in double-negative, as in 'I haven't got *nerrun*'

nast *n.* dirt; nastiness

nation *adv.*, *adj.* very. 'He wouldn't stop talking and it was *nation* annoying'. Probably from 'dam*nation*'

native *n.* (also **natif**) home or native country. 'I'm not sure what his *native* is' (NE HEREFS)

neal *v.* thin rods of hazel used to tie faggots are *nealed* in hot ashes to make them supple. From 'an*neal*'

near *adj.* stingy, mean

nearst *adv.* (also **neen**) near, next

neger *v.* (also **nauger**) to work very hard

neighbourhood *n.* (also **neighbourliness**) the phrase 'peace and good *neighbourhood*' is recited by the minister when he hands a Pax Cake to members of his congregation on Palm Sunday (SELLACK). The same phrase is also found on many church bells in Herefordshire

nesh *adj.* (also **neish, neshe**) 1. delicate, sensitive, tender, poor in constitution (LLANWARNE); 2. afraid of discomfort, cowardly (STAUNTON-ON-WYE)

nettle-bird *n.* willow warbler

nettle-creeper *n.* whitethroat (bird) (ROSS)

nettle in, dock out (also **ettle**) a charm chanted by children when using a dock leaf to ease a nettle-sting

new year's gifting *v.* the practice, by children, of visiting houses to solicit a new year's gift (N HEREFS)

nibby *n.* (also **nobby**) 1. a foal or colt (N HEREFS); 2. a term of endearment for a small child

nibs *n.* (also **nibbs**) parts of a scythe: the two hand-grips which are held to the *sned* by rings and *clets*

nice few *n.* an appreciable amount or number of. 'You got a *nice few* sheep there'

nichel *n.* a person who pays nothing

nicker *v.* 1. to neigh (horses); 2. to snigger

nidget *n.* a pronged instrument like a *horse hoe* (W HEREFS)

nighst *adj.*, *adv.* anywhere near; nearby

night churr *n.* nightjar (bird)

nile *n.* (also **hile, ile, knile**) generally the shorter, striking part of a flail used in threshing; rarely refers to the longer part, or handstaff (ASHPERTON, N HEREFS)

ninetedum *n.* corruption of 'anointed one'

ninny-pokin *n.* a stupid person (N HEREFS)

ninted *adj.* anointed, in a bad sense; mischievous

nip wir *n.* a buzz and a slap, triggered by a bee or wasp coming close. 'They come round my hat *nip wir*'

nisgal *n.* (also **niscal, nisgel, nisgul, niskin, nizgal, nurk**) 1. the youngest, smallest or weakest of a litter, of pigs, puppies etc. (from the Anglo-Saxon *nesc* or *hnesc* meaning delicate); 2. sometimes used in an uncomplimentary way for a small or weedy man; 3. the son kept longest at home, from 'nest gull' (LEOMINSTER, KENTCHURCH)

nist *n.* nest

no fear an expression of surprised disbelief, akin to 'no way!' 'Old George be dead? – *no fear*!'

no how (also **no road, no ways**) in no way; not at all

Noah and his wife *n.* lungwort (plant)

nob *n.* a young colt

nobble *n.* (also **hobble, obble**) a quandary or state of confusion or indecision. 'It's put me in a right *nobble*'

nobble-peg *n.*, *adj.* one who is stupid, not bright; no head piece. 'You won't get any sense out of that *nobble-peg*'

nobby *n.* endearing term for 1. a colt, akin to 'puss' for a cat; 2. a small child

nockerlated *adj.*, *v.* inoculated

no gift *adj.* stupid, not quite there

noggerly *adj.* thrifty. 'She was ever a *noggerly* one'

noggs *n.* (also **nibs**) the two handles of a scythe (W HEREFS)

nogman *n.* a clumsy, awkward, fumbling workman

noise *n.* quarrel, a scolding

none *n.* (sometimes pronounced to rhyme with 'own') no time. 'I was busy and had *none* for him'

nonsical *adj.* nonsensical

nooze *n.* a noose, a slip-knot

nope *n.* bullfinch (from its call)

nor *conj.* than. 'She's no better *nor* you'

north eye *n.* a good look-out; a sharp eye

nose *v.* to smell. 'Can you *nose* burning?'

not enough to poison a snipe very little indeed (a snipe is apparently ill-provided with entrails and is said to be very easily poisoned)

nouker *n.* a sharp one, a clever person

novist *n.* a novice or beginner

now just (also **now jest**) used in place of 'just now'. 'She was here *now just*'

nub *n.* 1. a lump, typically small. 'A *nub* of coal'; 2. a great, stout person. 'He's a great *nub* of a lad'

nurped *adj.* (also **nurped up**) starved with cold, freezing

nurpin *n.* a little person

nurra one *pron.*, *n.* never a one, nobody

O

oaf *n.* (also **ouph**) a strong insult. The derogatory phrase 'he's a prodigal half *oaf*' is the bitterest insult imaginable

oaken *adj.* made of oak

oarfood *n.* nightshade used as tonic for pigs and horses

oarup *n.* hogweed (WHITCHURCH)

oath *v.* to swear. 'Don't you *oath* at me!'

obbutty lantern *n.* a hollowed-out turnip with a candle inside (E HEREFS)

obligate *v.* 1. oblige. 'I'm *obligated* to you'; 2. engage. 'I've been much *obligated* with the lambing today'

oblionker *n.* 1. a child's name for a conker; 2. a game of conkers. The first player to say, 'obli, obli, onker, my first conker' has the right to strike first with his conker, and the game continues until one of the conkers is smashed

obstropolous *adj.* obstreperous, rowdy, disruptive

ockerd *adj.* (also **okard, okkerd**) 1. awkward, contrary (of things, weather); 2. awkward, obstinate, hasty-tempered, argumentative or bloody-minded (of people)

oddmark *n.* (also **oddment, off-going crop**) 1. a one-third part of a farm which the outgoing tenant may claim to sow with wheat etc. This crop had to be 'taken to' by the incomer just before the harvest; 2. more generally, 'the portion of an arable farm which, in the customary cultivation of a farm, is applied to a particular crop' (GCL)

oddments *n.* bits and pieces; odds and ends

odds *n.*, *v.* (also **odze**) 1. a difference; 2. to alter, adjust, undo. 'Please could you *odds* my trousers for me?' (LLANWARNE)

off-ta-go (also **away-ta-go**) off he or she went. Used to describe with the least possible delay. 'It's midday now so *off-ta-go*'; 'He gave me the message and *away-ta-go*'. Sometimes used more loosely: 'finish up and *off-ta-go*'

offen *prep.* off. 'Get that load *offen* the waggon'

offer *v.* (also **offer up**) 1. to attempt ('don't *offer* to come back here again'); 2. to threaten ('he *offered* to punch me'); 3. to be inclined to ('his dog may *offer* to bite you'); 4. to test for a fit, either by holding something up in front of one or by superstition (S HEREFS)

ognall *n.*, *adj.* (**ognal, ognel**) 1. land or soil that is wet, heavy and difficult to work; soil that will not 'come down' 2. surly, disagreeable, stubborn (W HEREFS); 3. unsightly, ugly, unpleasant

oil *v.* to beat, thrash. 'He'll *oil* your hide'

olas *adj.*, *adv.* (also **olus**) 1. careless, carelessly (SUTTON ST NICHOLAS, E HEREFS); 2. listless, lazy

old Charley *n.* (also **old Lawrence**) used in two senses: 1. a man constantly straightening his back while working might be said to have *old Charley* or *old Lawrence* on his back; 2. a man in a sulky or spiteful mood might also be said to have *old Charley* or *old Lawrence* on his back

old-fashioned *adj.* resentful or unfriendly. 'He looked at me a bit *old-fashioned* like'

old ladies *n.* (also **old maids**) gadflies, horseflies (WESTON-UNDER-PENYARD)

old people *n.* (also **very old people**) earlier generations

old 'un *n.* the Devil

ollus *adv.* always

omen *n.* (also **ominy**) a fad or fanciful contrivance. 'It's just an *omen* of hers' (N HEREFS)

on *prep.* 1. in ('the hedge is a bit gappy *on* places'); 2. at ('I'll catch the bus *on* lunchtime'); 3. of ('that's kind *on* you'). *On* is often used before a pronoun ('take hold *on* it' = take hold of it). Also used in the phrase 'how are you *on* for ... ?' = have you had enough of ... ?

onaccountable *adv., adj.* very, extremely. '*I'm onaccountable* pleased to meet you'

oney *adj.* (also **ony, owny**) 1. lazy (E HEREFS, DILWYN); 2. out of sorts, unwell (N HEREFS)

onfriends *adj.* unfriendly, not on friendly terms

onkind *adj.* bad, unfavourable, unhealthy (man or beast)

ooched up *adj.* (also **urched up**) huddled up as from cold or sickness. 'I was *ooched up* waiting for the storm to pass'

ood *adj.* (also **'ooden**) wooden

ooden suttut *n.* a coffin, as in a wooden overcoat. *Suttut* from the French *surtout* = above all

oolet *n.* (also **oolat, oolut**) 1. owl, owlet; 2. fool (N HEREFS)

oolies *n.* hairy caterpillars. 'There's *oolies* on my cabbages'

'ooman *n.* (also **auld 'ooman, 'ooman-volk**) the wives of labourers, as referred to by their husbands (LEOMINSTER, W & NW HEREFS)

oont *n.* (also **hoont, unt, woont**) mole

oontitump *n.* mole-hill (AYLTON)

ooshuck *n., adj.* impetuosity, rush and scurry. 'He came at me all *ooshuck*'

'ooster *n.* (also **'oostershire**) Worcester; Worcestershire

oot! to the off side (E HEREFS). See Waggoner's calls, p. 178

open weather *n.* fair weather, when the ground is not bound by frost, and can thus be readily worked

opinion *v.* to believe, be of the opinion that. 'I've *opinion* to think he's a liar'

orchat *n.* (also **archat, archut, aul, ochut, orchut**) orchard

ordain *v.* to give orders. 'He *ordained* that I get the hay in' (KINGSTONE)

orl *n.* (also **arl, orle, orrel**) alder (tree)

orld *adj.* old. 'My *orld* yud fils like a *turmit*' = my old head feels like a turnip (E HEREFS)

ornary *adj.* 1. ordinary, as usual; 2. unwell, poorly

ort *v.* to sort over

orter *n.* otter (N HEREFS)

orts *n.* bits, worthless odds and ends, refuse. 'I've cleared those *orts* from the shed'

orup *n.* (also **oarup**) hogweed (WHITCHURCH)

oss *v.* to try to do well (said of a servant); to set about doing. 'You can see how hard she's *ossing*' (AYLTON)

otomy *n.* skeleton (from 'anatomy'). See *atomy*

ould *adj.* cross or strange (N HEREFS)

ourn *pron.* ours. 'All those fields are *ourn*'

out *adv.* fully. 'He's not *out* seven years old'

outen *prep.* out of

over *v., adv.* 1. to leap over ('the horse *overed* the fence') (ROSS); 2. very ('it's *over* hot today'); 3. compared with ('today is hot *over* yesterday')

over anunt *adj.* adjoining (GOLDEN VALLEY)

over the door out of doors. 'He was inside too long so I kicked him *over the door*'

overlight *v.*, *n.* (also **overnight**) 1. alight (e.g. from a horse or vehicle); 2. that part of the day at the close of the afternoon yet before twilight has fairly begun

overlooked *adj.* (also **overseen**) 1. bewitched, under a spell (W HEREFS); 2. mistaken

oxberry *n.* 1. black bryony (plant) (N HEREFS); 2. also used for white bryony

oxeye *n.* great tit (bird)

P

pa-rabble *n.* a cussing; a ticking off. 'Those blighters got a good *pa-rabble* from their schoolmaster'

pachetty *adj.* (also **patchetty**) denoting bad or variable health. 'I feel a bit *pachetty*' (ARCHENFIELD, LLANGROVE)

packful *adv.* comprehensively, absolutely. 'The rabbits have *packful* stripped my greens' (MON BORDER)

packman *n.* a pedlar or higgler

padding can *n.* tramps' lodging house (LEINTWARDINE)

paddle *n.* an iron-shod stick used to clean the mould-board of old wooden ploughs

paggel *v.* to mend, though not necessarily well (bodge); also applied to digging or fencing carelessly done

pane of ground *n.* plot of ground, or portion or division of a garden; a plot of vegetables

pank *v.* (also **polt**) to knock or shake down apples from a tree. 'They're *panking* apples down in the orchard'

panking-pole *n.* (also **fruit-lug**) a long pole for shaking apple and pear trees

parish lantern *n.* the moon

parjeter *n.* a plasterer and tiler
parjeting *n.* the plaster lining on the inside of a chimney flue; also used more generally for plaster coatings, usually applied to outer walls
parliament *n.* (pronounced 'par-li-a-ment') a garden privy
parnch *n., v.* 1. strictly, an animal's paunch, but also used for the inedible viscera; 2. to eviscerate as a butcher would. Sometimes used of cattle, sheep etc., but these are more usually 'dressed'. Rabbits are invariably *parnched*
parsed *v.* married. 'They were *parsed* last Saturday'
part *n.* used in the context e.g. of 'this afternoon or *part*' = sometime this afternoon
partickler *adj.* (also **pertickler**) specific, precise. 'I favour that *partickler* one' (LEOMINSTER, LLANWARNE)
particular *adj.* untrustworthy (chiefly said of animals). 'Mind that bull, he's a *particular* one'
partly *adv.* more than very. 'I'm *partly* tired' = exhausted; '*partly* true' = true in every respect
parwhobble *n., v.* 1. a conference; 2. to talk without pause
pass out *v.* to toll a bell at a person's passing. 'Go into the tower and *pass out* the bell'. Intricate customs existed for which bells to toll in which order and for how long, in order to denote the age and sex of the deceased
patchetty *adj.* variable in health (LLANGROVE)
patienate *adj.* (sometimes pronounced like 'passionate') patient, forbearing
pauson *n.* (also **possun**) the parson
pea-bining *v.* pea-picking (MON BORDER)
peaking *adj.* feeble or puny

peaky *adj.* (also **peeky**) 1. bashful; 2. in poor health; wan

peal-of-bells *n.* campanula (from the bell-shaped flowers)

peart *adj.* (also **peart, peartified, peert, pyurt**) 1. lively, in good spirits or health; 2. bright and sparkling, as spring water; 3. sharp, tart (to the taste); 4. the second stage of inebriation. See *starry-eyed*

peas-brush *n.* (also **pease brush, peas-eddis, pea-esh**) pea stubble, when harrowed or brushed

peasen *n.* (also **pazen, peazen, pesen**) peas (W HEREFS)

peck *v., n.* 1. '*pecking* with rain' = raining lightly (E HEREFS); 2. to hurl, pitch; 3. to tease ('stop *pecking* your little brother'); 4. to pick out with a pickaxe or stocker; 5. a pick, pickaxe; 6. a unit of volume equal to 2 gallons

peel *n.* (also **peal**) long-handled shovel for removing bread from a baker's oven (W HEREFS)

peep of day *n.* dawn (E HEREFS)

peerk *n.* (also **peark, perk, perks, peurch**) 1. a perch, a linear unit of measurement of 5 1/2 yards. For digging by piecework, the perch was 5 1/2 yards square. However, the perch sometimes varied according to local custom, e.g. with a perch sometimes being 7 yards when applied to hedging; 2. a perquisite, an additional payment

peg *n.* pig sty

pell-necked *adj.* a sheep that has got the wool off its neck, from the wool being peeled off (MONNOW VALLEY)

pelt *n.* 1. the skin of a sheep after the wool has been taken off; 2. the shorter (striking) part of a flail

pen-feathered *adj.* untidy, dishevelled, with the appearance of an old quill pen

pentis *n.* 1. a penthouse; 2. the shed attached to a smithy where the horses are shod; 3. a shed with a sloping roof attached to the side of a house; a lean-to

pepper and salt *n.* field wood-rush (plant)

pergy *adj.* (also **perky**) 1. obstinate, surly; 2. saucy, uncivil

perket hole *n.* a small pit by an open hearth into which the ashes were raked and periodically emptied, sometimes from outside the house to avoid dust

pert *adj.* (also **piert**) brisk, in good health

perty *adj.* (also **ourty, pirty, purty, puttee**) pretty

peruse *v.* specifically to explore fields or woods (N HEREFS)

pessum *n.* the stems or stalks of peas; pea haulm

peth *n.* bread crumb

pharisees *n.* (pronounced 'fairisees') fairies (N & W HEREFS)

physic *n.*, *v.* a laxative medicine, or to treat with such

pick *v.* to glean

picklock *n.* in Herefordshire, the most valuable class of wool was known as *picklock* (the best *locks* being *picked*)

pie-finch *n.* (also **pierinch, pink, pinkin**) chaffinch (N HEREFS)

piece *n.* 1. a field or enclosure, often forming the second element in a place-name (e.g. Parson's *Piece*); 2. can be applied to animals or people, sometimes contemptuously or negatively. 'He's a nasty *piece*'

pig-meat *n.* the parts of the pig eaten before other parts of the animal are salted down; unsalted meat

pig-sty beef *n.* bacon (WIGMORE)

piggin *n.* (also **noggin**) a wooden quart used for carrying milk or toast and cider to workmen (ASHPERTON)

pigscot *n.* (also **pig's cott**) pig sty

pike *n.* (also **pikel, pikle**) pitchfork, hayfork (S & N HEREFS)

pikes *n.* the short furrows or the area covered by them, unavoidable in ploughing

pill *n.* a small creek, capable of holding barges for loading or unloading (from the Welsh *pil* = creek)

pimmerose *n.* (also, **pimerosen, pimrosen, pimmyrosen**) primroses

pinch-bar *n.* a crowbar (KENTCHURCH, LEOMINSTER)

pincushions *n.* field scabious (plant)

pine-end *n.* the gable end of a house

pinionated *adj.* (also **pinianated**) obstinate, opinionated, conceited

pins *n.* long, sharp, hard needles (MON BORDER)

pinsons *n.* (also **pinchers**) pincers

pip *n., v.* 1. the blossom of the cowslip; 2. 'To *pip* cowslips' = to pull the blossom from the stalks for making wine

pishty *adj., n.* 1. rubbishy, useless, of little value; weakly, poorly, worn out, e.g. of an animal ('a *pishty* old cow'); 2. a term applied to a dog when the speaker doesn't know its name (like 'puss' for a cat); a pet name for a puppy

piss-a-bed *n.* coltsfoot or dandelion, said to have diuretic properties (in the Pyrenees the dandelion is known as *piss-en-lit*: literally 'piss in bed')

pitch *n., v.* 1. a point. 'I always make a *pitch* of getting there early'; 2. a steep hill, generally on a road (used in place-names); 3. to pave, particularly with cobblestones; 4. to throw up or on, as hay onto a waggon (ROWLSTONE); 5. to settle, of snow. 'The snow is starting to *pitch*'

pitch-eyed *adj.* of broad beans, so ripe that the pods have developed black spots

pitchats *n.* broken china, glass etc. (possibly a corruption of 'potsherds')

pitched *adj.* cobbled, made of cobbles

pitching *n.* paths or yards made of picked field-stones laid on soil (PEMBRIDGE)

pithering *v.* 1. fussing about, fidgeting; 2. pestering, as flies etc. (ROSS, GLOS BORDER)

place *n.* a house with a small quantity of land attached

plaching *v.* pleaching; laying an old hedge

plain *adj.* unassuming, friendly in manner, unaffected. 'He's a *plain* sort'

plant *n.* a cabbage ('*plant* leaves' = cabbage leaves)

planted *v.*, *adj.* wheat is 'sown', but corn is always *planted*

platch *v.* (also **plash**) to pleach (lay) a hedge (W HEREFS)

playing on *v.* an expression generally used to describe birds (or occasionally rabbits) damaging crops. 'The sparrows are *playing on* the corn' (GOLDEN VALLEY)

playing war *v.* kicking up a fuss (MON BORDER)

pleacher *n.* (also **playcher, plasher**) in laying a hedge, a *pleacher* is the live growth partly cut through and laid, or '*pleached* down'

please to the 'to' is used where ordinarily it would be omitted. '*Please to* come over for supper'

pleck *n.* (also **plock**) a plot of ground, specifically a small meadow, roughly equivalent to a croft. The word is often used in connection with a name (Jenny's *Pleck*, Pepper *Plock* etc.)

plim *adv., adj., v., n.* (also **plimmer**) 1. very, completely; 2. smoothly; 3. to swell or fill up with food, to plump up (NW HEREFS, MON BORDER); 4. to let down a plumb line; 5. upright, perpendicular; 6. a plummet

plough *n.* a fall. 'I had a fearful *plough*' (NW HEREFS)

plug *v.* to hull (strawberries)

plump *v., n.* (also **flump**) to fall heavily, to flop down; a heavy fall

poche *v.* (also **pooch**) to prick a hole in anything; to '*poche* ground' is to tread it when wet

podge builder *n.* a jobbing builder employed for rough repairs (*podge* a corruption of 'bodge')

poi! poi! poi! call to cattle. See Calls to animals, p. 177

poke ridden *adj., v.* (also **poken-ledden, puck ledden**) 'spook-ridden', haunted; led astray by fairies (W HEREFS)

pole pitching *v.* setting up poles in a *hopyard*

pole ring *n.* (also **polering**) a ring that holds the blade of a scythe to the *sned* (handle)

polly ann *n.* polyanthus, a common cottage garden flower

polt *v., n.* (also **pote, poult**) 1. to knock apples from a tree; 2. to thump; a thump or hard knock (ROSS); 3. a push with the hand (W HEREFS)

pomace *n.* (also **pommey**) pulp, in cider-making; apples crushed to a pulp for the purpose of cider-making

ponger *v.* to wander

poon *v., n.* (also **poun, pun**) 1. to strike, as with a fist; to beat down; to knock, as on a door 2. to puddle clay

poor man's weather glass *n.* scarlet pimpernel (flower). So-named as the flowers only open when the sun shines

poplen *n., adj.* (also **poplern**) poplar tree; made of poplar

poppy *adj.* said of a man who wants to pass as a gentleman. 'He's a *poppy* one dressed in that get-up'

pot *n.* a local measure (more particularly in Worcestershire) containing 4.5–5 *pecks* of fruit or vegetables

pot fruit *n.* 1. edible fruit fit for sale and not for cider; 2. dessert apples

potato bury *n.* (also **potato stack, potato tump**) a heap of potatoes stored under soil to prevent frost damage

potch around *v.* to fiddle about

pother *v.* 1. to stir up (e.g. as of a wasps' nest); 2. to shake or poke (e.g. apples off a tree); 3. to squabble

pothering pole *n.* a long pole with a hook on the end used to shake down fruit, particularly cider apples

poultnessing *v.* poulticing (treating e.g. an inflamed area of skin with a poultice)

pound *v., n.* 1. to aid, to help or give assistance ('give me a *pound* with folding these sheets'); 2. a pond ('mill *pound*' was a commonly used phrase for a mill pond across Herefordshire)

pound-stakle *n.* the floodgates of a pond, or the post and frame which support them

pout-stakle *adj.* spirit-led, as if by a will-o'-the-wisp (from the Welsh *pwca* = a fiend or goblin)

poutch *v.* to pout

povey *n.* owl

power *n.* (also **poweration**) a great quantity or number. 'A *power* of people' = a large crowd (W HEREFS)

powse *n.* pulses, beans, peas etc.

prawl *v.* to stitch roughly, as in closing a sack (e.g. a *hop-pocket*); to patch or mend clothes; to cobble (N HEREFS)

pre-entry *n.* 'a right for an incomer in a February 2nd tenancy to enter on to the stubble to plough the land after November 1st, and also a right for stable room for two horses and a room for the ploughman' (WL)

pretty bobbish *adj.* very well (in reply to 'how are you?')

pretty fair *adj.* an understatement for a lot. 'We had a *pretty fair* amount of rain' = we had a lot of rain

pretty well of a fair quantity, a sufficiency. 'We've had *pretty well of* fruit this year' = plenty of fruit

pricked *adj.* sour (*pricked* cider is sour or bitter cider)

pride of the morning *n.* a slight early shower or mist (MUCH MARCLE)

prill *n.* a small brook; a purl (a twisting flow) in a stream (from the Welsh *prill* = rill)

pr'ill *adj.* abbreviated form of 'pretty little' (MON BORDER)

pritchell *n.* 1. a spike; 2. the membrum virile (penis)

prodigal *adj.* proud, in a derogatory sense

promiscuously *adv.* accidentally, by chance

prompt *adj.* fresh and jumpy, as a horse etc.

proper *adj.* 1. nice. '*Proper* job, that'; 2. real. 'A *proper* fool'

puck *v.* past tense of the verb 'to pick'. 'He *puck* it up'

pudduts *n.* 1. a baby's feet; 2. the paws of kittens or puppies

pue *n.* the udder of a cow

pug *v.* 1. to tug or pull (especially of hair); 2. to take out the tiny feathers left after poultry plucking; 3. to '*pug* a rick' of hay is, after thatching, to pull all of the loose ends from the sides, leaving it all neat and tidy

puggled *adj.* dumbfounded, mesmerised (N HEREFS)
puggy *adj.* tangled. 'My knitting's all *puggy*'
pulfin *adj.* fat. 'He's grown to be a great *pulfin* lad'
pull *n.* a payment on account. 'I asked my boss for a *pull*' (WHITCHURCH)
pulver *v.* to pilfer
pum-trow *n.* a pump trough
pumtree *n.* part of an old-fashioned hand-pump to a well, made from a bored-out elm log
punishment *n.* pain, in a general sense. 'My toothache has been giving me great *punishment*'
punk *n.* a knot cut from a crab apple tree
punning *n.* a beating. 'I gave him a good *punning*'
pure *adj.* well or sound in health (SUTTON ST NICHOLAS); free from disease
purgatory *n.* the ashpan under an open grate. 'Empty that *purgatory* for me' (UPPER SAPEY)
purgy *adj.* 1. cross, surly, quarrelsome; 2. stuck up
purpose *adj.* special, e.g. 'a *purpose* journey' = a special journey; one with a specific purpose or aim
purr! purr! call to turkeys. See Calls to animals, p. 177
puss *n.* a hare
put about *v.*, *adj.* to worry, vex or annoy; worried, irritated
put it to go *v.* (also **put to go**) to make it function, to repair or adjust (usually of machinery or implements)
puther *adj.*, *n.*, *v.* 1. hot and bothered. 'She's all of a *puther*'; 2. a cloud of smoke or dust; 3. to poke about, to stir a fire
puthery *adj.* hot, close (of weather) (S HEREFS)

Q

quabbed *adj.* flattened. 'My crops were *quabbed* by the rain' (WHITCHURCH)

quabble *n.* confusion

quack *v.* (also **queeck**) squeeze (NW HEREFS). 'Give it a quick *quack*'

quakers *n.* 1. stitchwort; 2. quaking grass (KENTCHURCH)

quank *v.*, *adj.* 1. to subdue; 2. still, quiet

quar *n.*, *v.* quarry

quarly *adj.* 1. always ailing or unwell; 2. fretful, agitated

quarter time *n.* quarantine (N HEREFS)

quat *n.*, *v.* (also **quot**) 1. a pimple or raised spot (ROSS); 2. to squat or crouch down

queek *v.* to press or squeeze down

Queen Anne's lace *n.* wild parsley

queenie-o-kokie-o *n.* a children's game (KINGSTONE)

queen's needlework *n.* valerian (plant)

quell *v.* of a hen, crushing her chicks in the nest

quick *n.*, *adj.* 1. young hawthorn; 2. a hedge of thorn; 3. quick-tempered

quiet *adj.* well-behaved, civil

quietly *adv.* gradually, steadily. 'She's getting better *quietly*'

quilt *v.* to swallow. '*Quilt* your medicine down'

quinel *n.* (also **quinnett**) of a scythe, a metal wedge passed between the lower ring and the *sned* holding the *grass nail* in place; the wedge or nail fastening the blade to the handle of a scythe

quire *v.* to inquire, to query. Also, the phrase 'to *lay quirence*' = to inquire

quist *n.*, *adj.* (also **queest, queis, quice, quist**) 1. a collared dove or wood pigeon; 2. quaint, queer, odd. There is an old Herefordshire saying: 'thee bist a queer *quist*' = you're an odd fellow (W HEREFS)

quitch *n.* couch grass

quithering *v.* talking or chattering low; whispering. 'Stop your *quithering* and speak up' (N HEREFS)

quob *n.*, *adj.* a bog, miry ground; quicksand; a shaking bog. 'I lost a boot in the *quob*'

quobby *adj.* swampy, marshy, water-logged. Wet ground that heaves when walked upon is *quobby* or 'all of a *quob*'. The word can also be applied e.g. to blancmange

quop *v.* to throb with pain. 'It *quops* something awful'

R

rack *n.* (also **rackway**) a rut in the road (S HEREFS); a path or roadway full of ruts; a narrow track or path

raddle *n.* red colouring used in marking sheep (N HEREFS). There is a red-soiled hill near St Michael's, Tenbury called 'The *Raddle* Bank'

Radnorshire pheasant *n.* thrush (MUCH BIRCH)

raer *adj.* (also **rear**) rare, underdone (as eggs or meat)

ragamuffin *n.* long-tailed tit

ragging *v.* playing on. 'I *ragged* on the ricks' (MON BORDER)

rain-bird *n.* green woodpecker

rainified *adj.* like rain; inclined to rain. 'It's a *rainified* out'

raisty *adj.* rancid, as bacon kept too long

raith *n.* (also **rait**) weeds, sticks or straw and other rubbish in a pool or running water

rammily *adj.* (also **rommily**) 1. tall and rank (e.g. grass); 2. leggy, loose, ill put together (e.g. animals, livestock)
rampagious *adj.* riotous; ill-disposed
ran thread *n.* whitey-brown thread used in strong sewing
randyrow *n.* a disturbance, commotion, uproar
rangle *n.*, *v.* a wound or fester; a wearisome pain (ORCOP)
rascally *adj.* 1. agonising, excruciating ('a *rascally* pain') (GOLDEN VALLEY); 2. excessive, deceptive, unreliable by defect or in action ('that waggon-load was *rascally* heavy'; 'that wheel's a might *rascally*')
ratch *n.* a subsoil consisting mainly of stone and gravel mixed with clay
rathe *adj.* early. 'A *rathe* brood of chicks' = an early brood
ratlin *n.* the smallest pig in a litter; the runt (N HEREFS)
rattle *n.* noise, often used of angry or argumentative conversation. 'They were making a great *rattle*'
ravvy grass *n.* raffia
reaming *adj.* very fine, superb. 'It's sunny and cloudless and *reaming* out'
rean *n.* (also **reen**) an open furrow; the interval between the ridges of ploughed ground. When there is no necessity for such drainage, the ridges are much wider and are called *lands*
rear up *v.* to bring up. 'He was *reared up* by his uncle'
reasons *n.* senses. 'He's out of his *reasons*'
reasty *adj.* (also **raisty**) rancid
reck staddle *n.* rick stool
recruit *v.* to mend, particularly a gate (N HEREFS)
reech *v.* to retch, vomit

reed *n.* the womb of a cow. 'She's thrown her *reed*' = she has a prolapse of the womb (PEMBRIDGE)
reek *v.* to cough
reeking *adj.* (also **reeksy**) restless, high spirited, full of energy, particularly of animals (N HEREFS)
reeves *n.* clusters (heavily laden). 'The plums are dangling in great *reeves*'
remember *v.* remind. '*Remember* me of it' (GOLDEN VALLEY)
remetic *n.* an emetic (something that causes vomiting). 'A *remetical* man' was sometimes used for a doctor
repping-hook *n.* (also **reppin-'uck**) reaping hook (W HEREFS)
resevoy *n.* reservoir
reynolds *n.* fox (a confusion of 'Reynard')
rheumatics *n.* (also **screwmatics**) rheumatism. 'She's got a nasty case of the *rheumatics*'
rick barton *n.* (also **rick barten**) fold yard (CANON FROME)
rid *n.* earth removed from the top of a quarry
rides *n.* several tree trunks growing out from one root (MON BORDER)
ridding *v.* tillering
riddings *n.* 1. the old or dead wood and brush first removed or cast out before a hedge is pleached; 2. excrement
riddle *n.* sieve
ridiculous *adj.* 1. scandalous and disgraceful (TRETIRE); 2. morally wrong
riff *n.* a skin disease
ring-beetle *n.* a wooden mallet strengthened with iron bands, used for driving wedges into wood etc. See *beetle*

rinnock *n.* the smallest pig in a litter; the runt (ROSS, THE FOREST OF DEAN). See *ratlin*

ripe *n.* (also **rip, rype**) a tapering square-sectioned piece of ivy-wood kept smeared with a mixture of lard and brick dust, used to give the final sharpening to a scythe blade; a four-sided strop for fine sharpening (W HEREFS)

ripping *adj.* sharp, cutting (of frost or cold)

ripple *n.* a small coppice, or thicket of underwood

rise *v.* to lift, raise. 'We're *rising* our spuds this week'

road *n., adv.* the right way or manner of doing anything. 'That's not the *road* to do it'; 'any *road*' = anyhow, anyway

roamish *adj.* 1. smelling or tasting unpleasantly (TRETIRE); 2. active, adventurous, restless

robble *adj., n.* in confusion, a tangled mass, used only in connection with soft materials. 'She left the bedclothes all of a *robble*' (BRAMPTON BRYAN)

rochlis *n.* rattle. 'He's got a nasty *rochlis* in his chest'

rollick *v.* (also **rollock**) to romp in an irregular, wayward fashion, like a puppy or a child

ronk *adj.* (also **ronkish**) 1. rank, rancid; 2. rotten, as timber; 3. growing luxuriantly; far gone in growth; 4. spirited, mischievous; 5. sexually desirous; 6. obstreperous, rowdy

root *v.* to rut

roozle *v.* (also **roosle**) of hens, birds etc. 1. to dust bathe ('the hens are *roozling* in the yard'); 2. to shelter ('the hen is *roozling* her chicks', i.e. under her feathers)

ropy *adj.* stringy, poor (of vegetables or cider)

ross *n.* a morass or low-lying area of wet ground (from the Welsh *rhos* = moor)

rot *n.* rat

rotter *n.* ratter. 'That dog's a good little *rotter*' (W HEREFS)

rough *n., adj.* 1. working clothes. 'Go upstairs and change out of your *rough*'; 2. poorly; in poor condition (cattle)

rough but kind *adj.* not yet well but getting better

rough music *n.* the dissonant banging of pans etc. made to express disapproval at the house of an immoral couple

roughet *n.* (also **ruffit**) rough ground; ground overgrown with bracken, briars, bush or scrub etc. (S HEREFS); a rough, breaky meadow (ARCHENFIELD)

rouk *n.* (also **rowk,** N HEREFS; **rout, rowt,** S HEREFS) a rut

roust *v.,* n. (also **rouse, rowe, rowsel up, rowst, rowstle**) 1. to stir up, to mix vigourously; to bestir oneself, to kick up one's heels. 'The cows are *rousting* up in the top field' (S HEREFS); 2. a stir, a mixing up. 'Give it a good *roust*'

row up *v.* ('ow' pronounced as in 'cow') 1. to rake hay into rows; 2. to stir up

rowcast *adj., n.* roughcast (a form of render coat)

rowing *n.* (also **rowings, rowins**) ('ow' pronounced as in 'cow') the short straw, weed seeds and other rubbish separated and thrown from the threshing box (N HEREFS)

rowsel up *v.* to stir up in one's mind

roxy *adj., vb.* of fruit going rotten over-ripe; to soften, decay

rubber *n.* a round sharpening-stone, or rough sandstone, used for sharpening scythes or hooks

ruck *n.* 1. a crease or fold (TRETIRE); 2. a rut; 3. a heap. 'A *ruck* of *mawn*' = a heap of peat

ruckle *v., n.* to rumple or crease

ruckled *adj.* creased or wrinkled

rudge *n.* a ridge in a ploughed field
ruggle *v.* (also **ruggle on**) to struggle (on) (LEOMINSTER)
ruggles *n.* small bells worn by Morris dancers at the knee
rull *v.* to roll (W HEREFS)
rullin drunk *adj.* rolling drunk (very drunk)
rummeldy *adj.* bent and tangled to such a degree that it cannot be rectified (used to describe less pliable materials than *robble*) (BRAMPTON BRYAN)
rump *n.* a young rabbit (KENTCHURCH)
rumpled skein *adj.*, *n.* anything that is in great confusion from being badly kept
run agin *v.* to meet by chance. 'Guess who I *run agin*'
run for it *v.* to try for something that one is unlikely to get; akin to 'whistle for it'. 'He can *run for it* all he likes' = he can try all he likes (MON BORDER)
run his word *v.* to go back on his word (LLANGARRON)
rundel *n.* (also **rundle**) a (hollow) pollarded tree (N HEREFS)
runted *adj.* underdeveloped, stunted (N HEREFS)
rusty *adj.* 1. rancid; 2. intractable

S

sa *v.* save. 'Thirty *sa* one is twenty-nine'
sacrament shilling *n.* 'a shilling that has formed part of the offertory at a Communion service. It was believed that if a sufferer from epilepsy wore one on a ribbon about their neck, it would help towards a cure. The coin had to be paid for in pence collected from 12 donors' (WL)
sad *adj.* heavy, doughy (of cakes and pastry)
saffern *n.* autumn crocus, from which saffron is derived

sallat *n.* (also **sallet**) salad of herbs

sally *n.* 1. sallow, willow or a bough thereof; 2. the woolly grip (the lower end) of a church bell rope

sally bed *n.* a willow plantation

sally withs *n.* (also **weathes**) from willow, used in orchards for binding faggots

salty *adj.* 1. expensive, overpriced, unreasonable. 'Ten pounds is a bit *salty*, isn't it?'; 2. littered with expletives (of language)

sample *n.* portion, part

sapey *adj.* (also **sapesy**) 1. soft due to being full of sap (sappy); 2. of things which, being naturally firm in texture, have become softened by deterioration

Sarah *n.* a hare or mode of address to a hare. Throughout the country, the word *puss* is more generally used

sarcle *v.* to weed corn fields (CANON FROME)

sartin sure! of course!; to be sure!; certainly!

sarvant sir *n.* old men, in the late nineteenth century, when meeting a gentleman, would often use this form of salutation, taking off their hats and bowing low

satin flower *n.* greater stitchwort

sauce *v.* to abuse. 'He *sauced* me something terrible'

savage *n.* butcher's broom (plant), used by waggoners on their horses in carefully regulated doses as a tonic and stimulant. Reputed to be dangerous if used to excess

sawney *adj.*, *n.* foolish; a fool. See *simony*

scallenge *n.* (also **skallange, skallynge, scallage**) lychgate or the bench therein at the entrance to the churchyard (CANON PYON, STAUNTON-ON-WYE)

scallenge-block *n.* a mounting block (for mounting horses) near the churchyard gate

scambling *adj.* 1. sprawling; 2. rushed, makeshift. 'A *scambling* job' = a job done too hurriedly

scarified *adj.* terrified

scarify *v.* 1. to break up the ground; 2. to scare, to terrify

scholard *n.* an educated person

sckelt *adj., n.* worthless; a worthless thing

sclem *v., n.* to steal; a sneak-thief, a wily pilferer (e.g. a poacher or a thieving cat). The term was often applied specifically to animals: a calf that takes milk from other than its own mother is *sclemming* (BREDWARDINE)

scoat *v.* to rush, hurry along. '*Scoat* along with you!'

scog *v.* to boast. 'You should have heard him *scog* about it'

scogger *n.* boaster

scogging *adj.* boastful

scolloping *adj.* draggling, bedraggled, wet and dirty

scoot *n., v.* 1. a division or part of a garden (EYE); a swath or area of grass (N HEREFS); 2. to slide (KENTCHURCH)

score *n.* a measure of weight for pigs

scorting *adj.* scornful; high and mighty

scot *n.* a public house account or tab. 'Your *scot* is overdue'

scotch hands *n.* wooden butter pats

scote *n.* a dragstaff (a rear-mounted pole, for e.g. a cart, to halt undue backward movement)

scout *v., n.* a cricketing term for fielding near the boundary

scoutch *n.* (also **scutch, coutch**) couch grass

scowl me brow *v.* to peer intently; to study with great concentration

scowles *n.* the workings of old mines since overgrown with vegetation, thus potentially concealed

scrabble *v.* (also **scrobble**) to scramble

scran *n.* food. 'I'm off home for a bit of *scran*' (ROSS)

scrat *v.*, *n.* (also **scrattle,** W HEREFS) 1. to scratch; 2. to try hard or work hard; to work against time; 3. to rush, hurry (S HEREFS); 4. a miserly, stingy person

scratchings *n.* (also **scrutchings**) the refuse in the form of crispy pieces left after the rendering down of fat (usually pork), later popularised as a bar snack

scratter *n.* 1. one who *scrats*; 2. a machine taking the place of a cider-mill, worked by hand or power to reduce cider-apples to pulp ready for pressing

scrawl *v.* to creep or crawl (KENTCHURCH, N HEREFS)

scrawling *adj.* slight. 'A *scrawling* frost' = a slight frost

screech *n.* (also **screecher, devil's screecher**) 1. the swift (bird); 2. also sometimes used for the mistle thrush

screwce *n.* a very small quantity (BRAMPTON BRYAN)

screwy *adj.* mean, niggardly (S HEREFS)

scribbling schoolmaster *n.* the yellowhammer, from the markings on its eggs which look like the scribblings made by a quill pen (E HEREFS)

scriggly *adj.* 1. mean (*screwy*); 2. too small. 'I couldn't read her *scriggly* handwriting'

scritch *v.* screech

scroudge *v.*, *n.* (also **scrouch, scrowge, scrudge**) to crush (old-fashioned, traditionally used by school masters); to press together, or make untidy

scrouse *v.* (also **scrout,** BRAMPTON BRYAN) rummage (ROSS)

scrowl *n.* a scrape, difficulty. 'I got myself in a *scrowl*'

scruffed *adj.* damaged, pulled out or torn. 'A magpie has *scruffed* the nest' (MON BORDER)

scrumps *n.* windfall apples (ROSS)

scud *n.* a slight, fleeting shower. 'It's just a *scud*'

scuffle *n.* (also **scuffler**) a horseshoe

scunny *n.* a rabbit (WIGMORE)

scutch *n.* cutch-grass (couch grass)

scuts *n.* (also **scutties**) rabbits (N & E HEREFS)

see *v.* find. 'I *see* it very hard' (ARCHENFIELD)

see! see back! to a horse, instruction to turn right. See Waggoners' calls, p. 178

seed *v.* past tense of verb 'to see'; saw. 'I *seed* him coming'

seedny *n.* a time of sowing the land

seeds *n.* (also **sids**) clover

seggen *adj.* made of *segs* (rushes)

seggs *n.* yellow flag iris (STAUNTON-ON-WYE)

segs *n.* rush (sedge). Chiefly the rush used for chair seats, but any water-logged meadow in which rushes grow may be described as *seggy*

selion *n.* 1. furrow; ridge and furrow (WELSH NEWTON); 2. sometimes found as the second part of a field-name (e.g. The Big *Selion*, LINGEN)

send *v.* 1. to see off; to accompany one for the purpose of seeing off. 'I must *send* my grandparents at the station' (S HEREFS); 2. to accompany on the road

set *v., n.* 1. to let or lease; to let a farm or land to a tenant (W HEREFS). A landlord *sets* a house; a tenant *takes to* a house; 2. seated. '*Set* at the table'; 3. bulbs for planting out

seven-coloured linnet *n.* the goldfinch (rare) (E HEREFS)
shabbing *n.* a quantity. Specifically, to have a *fair shabbing* of anything implies having an appreciable but moderate quantity (generally used in reference to fruit or other crops). Sometimes used in an ironical sense to imply an unusually large number or a very full crop
shamble *v.* to walk lethargically; to slouch along
shanna *v.* shan't
shantsyer *v.* (also **shantisyer, wunt yer**) won't you? '*Shantsyer* be at work today then?'; '*Shantsyer* have some?' (WORCS BORDER)
shape *n.* vulva
shard *n.* (also **shoard**) a gap in a hedge; an open place (ASHPERTON, GLOS BORDER). See *glat*
sharpish *adj.* considerable, significant. Almost identical to *smartish*, but more often used where pain is concerned
shatter out *v.* (also **shatter**) 1. ripe or over-ripe corn falling or bursting out from the ear is said to *shatter out*; to shed out; 2. friends falling out with one another may also be said to have *shattered out*
she *pron.* her, used as a direct or indirect object of the personal pronoun. 'We told *she* to hurry up'
sheal *v.* 1. to come cleanly and easily away from the outer covering, e.g. ripe nuts from their shells (BRAMPTON BRYAN); 2. to shell peas or beans; 3. to shed or scatter (a term used in ploughing) (ASHPERTON)
sheal board *n.* (also **shellboard, shell-board**) the mould-board of a plough
shealers *n.* (also **brown shealers**) ripe nuts

sheeler *n.* a machine used to extract the seed from clover (KENTCHURCH)

sheepskin drummer *n.* a slovenly-done job

sheep-stare *n.* (also **stare**) starling (used by Chaucer)

shelly *n.* chaffinch (bird)

shelterdy *adj.* affording shelter. 'A warm, *shelterdy* place'

shepherd's delight *n.* scarlet pimpernel (plant)

shespy *n.* a shoe-horn (from the French *chausse-pied* = shoe-horn) (STOKE EDITH)

shift *v.* 1. to move house; 2. to remove; to change. 'I'll *shift* myself' = I'll change my clothes; 3. 'To make *shift*' = to make do

shimmy *n.* (also **shift**) a chemise

shingling *n.* a sprinkling, as of fruit on a tree

ship *n.* sheep. 'Go get the *ship* in'

shippick *n.* (also **shippuck**) a pike, a pitchfork

shirgle *v.* shirk. 'He often *shirgles* his responsibilities'

shitten *adj.* embarrassed or shamefaced

shivering *n.* (of gravel etc.) a light sprinkling. 'I've thrown a *shivering* over that patch of ice'

shobbeler *n.* an old horse past heavy work and kept on the farm to do odd jobs or light work

shoddy *v.* to *shoddy* building-stones is to chisel the edges only (sometimes only the outside edges) straight and square, leaving the faces rough or only slightly worked

shoddying hammer *n.* a hammer used to *shoddy* stone, like a double-edged axe; used instead of a hammer and chisel

shoes *n.* boots as generally worn are often referred to as *shoes*; and shoes not coming above the ankle as *low shoes*

shoes and stockings *n.* bird's foot trefoil (plant)

shommaking *v.*, *adj.* 1. love-making; 2. idling, clumsy (ARCHENFIELD)

shop-window fuddle *n.* time spent gazing into shop windows but not buying anything; window shopping

shore back *v.* to hang or draw back, as a led horse

short gears *n.* the harness for the shaft or filler horse, i.e. bridle (*mullen*), collar and *hames* with tugs, cart-saddle, belly-band (girth) and crupper

shot *n.* a sum of money. 'I paid a goodly *shot* for it'

shoul *n.* a shovel

shown *v.* (also **shownd**) past tense of 'to show'

shrammed *adj.* suffering from the cold

shreek *n.* (also **shriek**) shrike (butcher-bird)

shuck *v.* past tense of 'to shake'. 'Go *shuck* that mud off!'

shuck the alf *v.* to play the fool. 'Don't *shuck the alf*!'

shucky *adj.* jarring, rough, uneven (e.g. of a bad road)

shud *n.*, *v.* 1. shed; 2. to take off, to leave off

shunna *v.* shall not. 'I *shunna* be going out'

shuppick *n.* a hayfork

shut *v.*, *n.* 1. to rid ('to get *shut* of' = to get rid of); 2. to empty ('to *shut* out' = to empty out); 3. to join, as in welding; 4. a shoot or spout of water

shut-link *n.* a split link or open link used for temporary repairs to a chain trace (ROSS)

sicking *v.* sighing (PIXLEY)

sidelands *n.* (also **sidelants, sidlands**) a steep hillside, or part of it; a *sideland* farm is a farm on the slope of a hill (GOLDEN VALLEY)

sideways *prep.* on the side of; in the direction of. 'They lived *sideways* Leominster'

sidling *adj.* (also **sideland, sideling, sidelong**) sloping, steep. 'The top field's too *sidling* for planting'

sids *n.* seeds

siers *n.* scions or shoots

sieu! sieu! ('*sieu*' to rhyme with 'stew') (also **si-ew! si-ew!, stew pig!, stew Jack!**) call for driving loose pigs. See Calls to animals, p. 177

sigh *adj., pron.* (also **sish**) such. 'Don't be *sigh* an idiot'

sight *n.* a large number. 'There's a *sight* of fine Herefords out on the meadow'

silent *n.* (also **silence**) asylum (TRETIRE)

silgreen *n.* (**silly-green, singreen**) house leek (plant) (KENTCHURCH)

silly *adj.* weak, poorly

sim *v.* to seem

simony *adj.* simple, unintelligent, mentally dull (after 'Simple Simon')

simple *adj.* unwell, weak (BRAMPTON BRYAN)

sin *v., prep., conj.* 1. past tense of 'to see'. 'I *sin* him coming over the hill'; 2. since

single out *v.* to thin out plants or roots

sinners *n.* sinews

sir *n.* (also **sirrah, sirry, surrey, surry**) a form of address that can be either familiar or contemptuous, probably from the old term 'sirrah' (N HEREFS)

siu! siu! (pronounced to rhyme with 'do') call to drive pigs. See Calls to animals, p. 177

skeart *adj.* scared

skeal *n.* (also **skeel**) 1. a shallow wooden bowl or tub; 2. a long-handled shovel or peel (BROMYARD)

skeer *n.* (also **skir-devil**) swift (bird)

skeg *n.* 1. the stump of a branch; 2. the hole or tear in a piece of cloth caused by contact with the stump or the sharp end of a branch

skein *n.* a great number (of people)

skelloping *v.* rushing around a field (cattle etc.) (N HEREFS)

skelt *v.*, *n.* 1. to roam, to wander off; 2. a vagabond, a worthless person

skerrier *n.* (also **scarifier**) a spring-tined harrow

skewer wood *n.* spindlewood, dogwood or elder

skid *n.* (also **skidpan**) the slipper on a cartwheel, a drag (to act as a brake)

skilling *n.* a roof slope (KENTCHURCH)

skim *v.* to plough a field very shallowly

skip *n.*, *v.* 1. a shallow basket made out of oak laths with a rounded bottom and ends (more commonly used in Shropshire); 2. a beehive made of straw 3. to run away

skippet *n.* (also **skuppet**) 1. a long-handled shovel with raised sides, particularly for use with hops in a *hop kiln*. The blade can be of wood, but also of e.g. canvas over a timber frame; 2. a small, flat shovel, also with raised sides on a long handle, but used for flat-bottoming narrow trenches or for handling mud (more commonly made with a metal blade)

skirme *v.* to mow lightly; to trim a crop or mow when the crop is light. 'He just wants you to *skirme* it' (MARDEN)

skith *n.* 1. a thin layer of snow. 'Just a *skith* of snow on the hill'; 2. a *skith* of rain = very light rain (BRAMPTON BRYAN)

sklem *v.* to steal slyly, applied almost solely to animals, particularly cats and dogs. 'The cat's *sklemmed* that fish you left on the side'

sklenn *n.* a greedy and indiscriminate feeder

slab *n.* (also **slob**) the rounded piece cut from a tree trunk when squaring it for timber

slad *n.* (also **slad pitch**) the hollow side of a hilly road; the bank (sometimes found in place-names: Cold *Slad* etc.)

slade *n.* a valley

slammockin *n.* a slattern

slang *n.* (also **slanget, sling, slingate, slinget**) a long, narrow strip of land or enclosure; a strip of field (N HEREFS). Possibly from the German *schlange* = snake. See *langet*

slart *v.* to stain. 'Those blackberries will *slart* your shirt'

slasher *n.* a hacker; a long-handled bill-hook for hedging

slat *v.* the past participle of 'to slit'

slatted *adj.* said of peas when the blossom has developed into pods

sleave *v.* to tear down (the branch of a tree etc.)

sleaving *n.* a twig or branch *sleaved* off

sleepy *adj.* soft, overripe (particularly in reference to pears). 'Them pears have gone *sleepy*'

slennocks *n.* strips. 'To cut *slennocks*' = to cut strips

slep *v.* past tense of 'to sleep'; slept

slepper *n.* a slipper (or brake wedge) on a cartwheel; a drag. See *skid*

slether *v.* to slither, slide. 'To *slether and slob*' = to slip and slide about (e.g. in thick mud, snow etc.)

slick *adj.* (also **slike**) 1. icy, slippery, slick (of roads etc.); 2. smooth, glossy (of animals) (N HEREFS)

slinger *n.* a thief; specifically 'one who steals cloth yarn or the like from clothiers, with a view to its being worked up or finished' (GCL)

slip *n.* an eight-week-old pig (GLOS BORDER)

slit *v., n.* to plough so that the furrows fall outwards and away from each other to form a *rean* is described as *slitting*. See *land*

sliving *n.* a slice cut off. 'Hand me a *sliving* of that cake'

slob *v.* to slide

sloen *n.* plural of sloe (blackthorn berry)

slommock *v., n.* (also **slommock about, slummock**) 1. to work with little will; to be lazy (N HEREFS); to slouch along; 2. a slattern; a woman or man untidy in dress

slommocky *adj.* (also **slummocky**) slovenly

slop *n.* a coarse brown overall (WIGMORE)

sludge *n.* a wet or muddy place

slurring *v.* sliding

slush *n.* 1. loose mud; 2. loose talk

slushy *adj.* 1. miry; 2. foul-mouthed

sly spring *n.* a spring that appears intermittently. 'A *sly spring* is wet then dry' (MON BORDER)

smacker *n.* a big thing. 'That fish were a *smacker*'

smackle *v., n.* to throw out sparks from a wood fire. 'See the way that fire *smackles!*' (ARCHENFIELD)

smart *adj.* 'A *smart* few' = a good many

smart arse *n.* knotweed (plant)
smartish *adv.* (also **sharpish**) quite considerably. 'That cut bled *smartish*'; 'It was raining *smartish*'
smirch *v., adj., n.* (also **smouch**) 1. to daub; 2. dirty; 3. stain
smock frock *n.* a labourer's strong hempen garment with shoulder lapels much gathered in and pleated (falling into disuse by the end of the nineteenth century)
smoozed *adj., v.* smoked
snaff *v.* to sniff noisily or scornfully
snag *n., v.* 1. a rough, projecting stump of a tree; 2. to tease; 3. to repeat the same thing several times
snaggle *v.* to notch or cut badly
snappers *n.* 1. stitchwort; 2. snapdragons (plants)
snarled *adj.* entangled. 'The ewe got *snarled* in the briars'
snatch *n.* a snack; a little meal; a bite between meals (MON BORDER). See *bait*
snawp *n.* a stinging blow; a smart tap on the head or other part of the body. 'Give him a *snawp* and wake him up!'
snawps *n.* foxgloves (plant)
sned *n.* (also **sneed, snid**) the shaft of a scythe (N HEREFS)
sness *v.* to sneeze. See *tussing*
snew *v.* past tense of 'to snow'. 'It *snew* hard last night'
sniffetting *v., adj.* sniffling. 'Stop your *sniffetting*' (ROSS)
sniping *adj.* sharp or biting, as of frost or wind
snirpt *adj.* (also **snurped**) pinched with cold; frozen
snite *v.* to blow one's nose. 'Give it a good *snite*'
snithing *n.* (also **sniving**) a swarm, infestation (W HEREFS)
snive *v.* to swarm (of mice etc.)
snob *n.* a cobbler, shoe repairer

snobbing *v.* tapping lightly, as a cobbler does when soling shoes; mending shoes (MON BORDER)

Snob's Row *n.* the name given, at the end of the nineteenth century, to a row of houses in Ross due to the number of shoe repairers dwelling there. Ross was famous for its boots from medieval times

snook *v.* past tense of 'to sneak'; stole, crept. 'He *snook* out before dawn'

snoosle *v.* (also **snoozle, snuzzle down**) 1. to snuggle down in bed (said to children) (N HEREFS); 2. to nestle under a sheltering wing or arm (ROSS). See *roozle*; 3. to creep

snorter *n.* a highly imaginative statement; a whopping lie. 'She told him a mighty *snorter*'

snorty *adj.* proud, haughty (N HEREFS)

snotty-berry *n.* the fruit of the yew tree; a yew berry

snow *n.* ('ow' pronounced as in 'cow') snow

snowler *n.* 1. a piece of bad news; a great disappointment or unfortunate occurrence; 2. a heavy blow, as on the head

snug *adj.* easily pleased

so *adj.* euphemism for pregnant. 'She's *so*' = she's pregnant

so as so long as, provided that. 'I don't care *so as* it's done'

so well as well; just as well. 'I might *so well* give up'

soak *n.* 'a green *soak* or a warm *soak* is a small spot of marshy ground, in which a spring rises, or which is kept moist during the winter by the action of water. It differs from a *gall*, as being generally a low hollow place, whereas a *gall* may be on a sloping bank' (GCL). See *sough*

sock *n., v.* 1. a ploughshare; 2. a hard blow with the hand; 3. to smack, hit

soft *adj.* foolish, in contrast to one who is 'hard-headed' and thus shrewd or wise

soldiers' buttons *n.* bachelor's buttons (cornflowers) (ROSS)

sole *n.*, *v.* 1. a collar of wood, put around the neck of cattle so that they can be attached to a *stelch* (post); 2. to bind or fasten cattle in their stalls

solid *n.*, *adj.* (also **solid man**) 1. one who is well-to-do or has money in the bank; 2. solemn; steady and serious

soller *n.* (also **sollar**) 1. an upper room; bedroom. 'Up the *sollers*' = upstairs (W HEREFS); 2. chamber nearest the sun

solomon *n.* a soft and easy job. 'He looked knackered so I gave him a *solomon*'

some odd *n.* usually refers to small coinage in an amount of money. 'It cost me five pounds and *some odd*'. Also refers to quantities more generally. 'Three hundred bags and *some odd*'

soople *adj.* supple

sore *adv.*, *adj.* 1. greatly, very great (in a bad sense). 'You were *sore* drenched by that storm'; 2. roguish. 'A *sore* fellow' = a rascal or rogue

sort about *v.* to search around. 'Go and *sort about* for it'

sough *n.* a small boggy spot, generally covered with green moss, on the eye of a spring (LLANWARNE)

sould *n.* soul

sour *adj.* 1. heavy, wet (of land); 2. sore; 3. disagreeable

sour sally *n.* sorrel (plant) (ROSS)

spadger *n.* (also **spadjuck**) house sparrow. 'The *spadgers* are bickering in the hawthorn' (from the Old Norse)

spaggled *adj.* ripped or torn, as the branch of a tree

spawl *n.*, *v.* (also **spawl off**) 1. a piece of unworked stone split off by using a *spawling-hammer*; 2. a splinter or piece of wood split off a tree or branch (KENTCHURCH); 3. to split or shear off forcibly (wood or stone); a tree bough splitting off at the trunk has *spawled* off

spawling-hammer *n.* a steel hammer, about 5lbs in weight, used to split a rough piece of stone

spede *n.* spade

speer *v.* to stare, peer. 'I caught him *speering* over the fence' (W HEREFS)

spet *v.*, *n.* spit

spile *v.*, *n.* 1. to spoil; 2. a small peg in the bung of a tapped barrel, to control the admittance of air

spill *n.*, *v.* 1. a sliver of wood, a splinter; 2. to splinter

spirtle *v.*, *n.* (also **spurtle**) spurt, sprinkle, splatter, splash

spit *n.*, *v.* 1. the depth of the blade of a spade; a spade depth. Single-digging is one *spit* deep; double-digging is two *spits* deep; 2. to drizzle; to spot with rain

spittle *n.* (also **spittal**) a spade or spade handle. *Spittle*-making was once a Herefordshire trade (W & S HEREFS)

splavin *n.* a conspicuous boil or wart etc. 'A great blotch of eruption' (GCL)

splite *n.* a laughing stock. 'You've made a *splite* out of me' (KENTCHURCH)

splotched *adj.* spotted, blotched, blotchy

sporrocks *n.* steel springs in boots (N HEREFS)

spottle *v.* to splash. 'I got *spottled* by that puddle'

sprag *adj.* (also **sprack, spract**) 1. lively, vigorous; 2. smart in appearance (ROSS); 3. quick-minded

spreck *adj.* spry, alert, tidy and in good order (akin to 'spick and span'). 'He's a *spreck* young lad'

spreed *v.* to spread (past tense: *sprod*). 'Go and *spreed* the muck'; 'He *sprod* the muck'

spreeder *n.* (also **spreader**) a crosswise piece of wood that prevents the traces of the fore-horses of a team from collapsing, or getting under the horses' legs (W HEREFS)

sprite *adj.* lively, as of a dog etc. 'He's getting on a bit but is *sprite* for his age'

sprowse *n.* the loppings of branches etc., used to fill a *glat* (hole) in a hedge

spud *n.* a grafting or draining tool

spurt *n., v.* 1. a potato shoot or sprout; 2. to sprout in general, but of potatoes specifically. 'The spuds are *spurting* well'; 3. to *spurt* potatoes = to rub off the *spurts* from old potatoes

squab *n.* a baby wood pigeon

squamble *v.* to scramble, over a hedge, wall etc. (N HEREFS)

square *adj.* well in health. 'I'm feeling more *square* now' (WELSH NEWTON)

squat *n., v.* (sometimes pronounced to rhyme with 'cat') 1. a rabbit's or hare's form (a sheltering dip in the ground); 2. a prop, shoe or skid (typically an oblong piece of wood with a handle) placed under a wheel to prevent the wheel from moving; 3. to prevent the movement of a wheel with a *squat* ('to *squat* the wheel') (WIGMORE)

squawk *v.* to squeal, to cry out

squeaker *n.* a swift (bird)

squeal-pig *n.* (also **squel-pig**) rough cider (MUCH MARCLE)

squelt *n.* (also **squilt**) a pimple; a lump which may come to a head (ROSS); an eruption on the skin; a raw wound. 'That's a nasty *squelt* you got there'

squit *n.* (also **squitter**) 1. nonsense, rubbish; useless, vapid conversation; 2. a derogatory term used by children. 'She's a silly little *squit*'; 'don't go listening to their *squitter*'

squitch *n.* quitch, couch grass

squob *adj.* settled down, as a rick

sriek *v.* (also **skriek**) to shriek

srimp *n.* shrimp

srink *v.* to shrink

srivelled *adj.* shrivelled

srub *n.* shrub

stack *n.* a flight of stone steps up to the upper floor, hayloft etc., on the outside of a farm building

stam *n.* (also **stom**) stem

stand *v.* (also **stand for, stand to**) 1. to act as a godparent, or as a sponsor (to a child); 2. (also **stand market**) to have a stall at a market; to attend a market regularly for the purpose of selling (ROSS)

stand back! instruction to horses to come back (E HEREFS). See Waggoners' calls, p. 178

stank *n., v., adj.* 1. a dam, or pool caused by a dam; 2. to dam, as of a brook; to flood by obstructing an outflow (typically used with '*back*': 'to *stank back*' = to form a small dam); 3. to clear rubbish from a ditch and pile it on a bank (GOLDEN VALLEY); 4. to staunch (e.g. the flow of blood); 5. cows overdue for milking are '*stanked up*'; 6. an old saying: '*Stank* afore it' = eat before drinking

star of Bethlehem *n.* greater stitchwort (plant)

stare *n.* (also **black steer, steer, steere**) starling (bird)

starky *adj.* (also **starchy**) said of stuff (material) that is hard to work with a needle (ARCHENFIELD)

starry-eyed *adj.* having had a little drink. The three stages of inebriety are: i) *starry-eyed* (slightly tipsy), ii) *peart* (fairly well-oiled), and iii) *dronk* (blind drunk)

start *v.* to flush in relation to game, rabbits etc., but also used in place of the verb 'to find' or 'to procure'. 'Go to the shed and *start* me that spanner'

starve *v.* to perish with cold (N HEREFS)

starve-crow farm *n.* very poor farming land

stayers *n.* stairs

stealing her nest *v.* said of a hen that lays her eggs away from the hen-house

steamer *n.* (pronounced 'stemmer') a traction engine

stean *n., v.* (also **steen**) 1. a large, open, glazed earthenware pot, typically used for preserving eggs or pickling meat; or for washing (from the German *stein*) (ASHPERTON); 2. 'To *steen* a well' = to line a well

steecker *n.* (also **sticker**) a stick used to stop a waggon or cart descending a hill

steeve *n.* 1. an ox; 2. also used for the pole attached to the collar between the oxen when at work

stelch *n.* an upright post to which the *sole* (a wooden collar for cattle) is attached by means of a *with* (a twisted band of wood, usually of willow)

stele *n.* (also **stale**) the wooden handle or shaft of a rake or pitchfork (LLANGARRON)

stemming *v.*, *adj.* said of those employed with agricultural steamers or traction engines (LINTON)

stetch *n.* the distinct areas into which a field is marked for ploughing

stew! (also **stoo!**) call used to drive pigs (GOLDEN VALLEY). See Calls to animals, p. 177

stick *n.*, *v.* 1. a tree grown for timber ('a good *stick*' = a good tree) (MON BORDER); 2. an oddball ('he's a queer *stick*'); 3. 'to go up the *stick*' = to lose one's temper (S HEREFS); 4. to hold one's opinion ('I *stuck* him out, despite what he said'); 5. 'to go *sticking*' = to search for dry pieces of wood for kindling (ROSS)

stiff *adj.* strong for his build. 'He's a *stiff* little man'

stipe *n.*, *adj.* a steep ascent on a road

stir-up Sunday *n.* 'the 25th Sunday after Trinity, so-called from the Collect for the day which begins 'Stir up, we beseech Thee, O Lord'. This was taken by housewives as a reminder that it was time to start making Christmas plum puddings' (WL)

stitch *n.* the slightest thing. 'She won't do a *stitch* to help'

stither *n.* a small bit of anything (N HEREFS)

stived *v.*, *adj.* concealed. 'Kept in too close a place' (FTH)

stock *v.* 1. to peck as a bird; *stocking* = pecking (MON BORDER); 2. to grub up a hedge ('to *stock* up a hedge') (N HEREFS); 3. to break up the ground; 4. to hoe up weeds with a *stocker*

stock-axe *n.* mattock

stock-eagle *n.* (also **stockeagle, stockeekle, stockicle, stock-hecle**) green woodpecker

stocker *n.* a mattock; a large hoe for earthing up potatoes or weeds

stoddle stones *n.* (also **staddles**) staddle stones (stone supports, sometimes mushroom-shaped, for a granary or rick, to keep the grain clear of vermin)

stoggle *n.* (also **stockel, stockeld, stoggerel**) a pollarded tree; an old gnarled tree with a large, misshapen head

stoggle oak *n.* (also **stoggledy oak**) one sprung from the stump of an oak, not from an acorn; one with a short, thick, lumpy trunk (MON BORDER)

stogwell *n.* a pollarded tree, not for timber (e.g. willow) that belongs to the tenant not the landlord (LLANWARNE)

stone horse *n.* a stallion

stonen *adj.* (pronounced with a short 'o') of stone (TRETIRE)

stonen stile *n.* a slab placed upright to form a stile

stood *v.*, *adj.* stopped, particularly referring to someone halting work. 'He downed his tools and were *stood*'

stook *n.* (also **stuck**) a group of sheaves

stop-glat *n.* literally a stop gap; brush etc. used to block a gap or *glat* in a hedge

storier *adj.* story-telling (used by children)

storm *n.* a quarrel (S HEREFS)

storm-bird *n.* green woodpecker

storm cock *n.* (also **stormcock, storm screech**) mistle(toe) thrush (so-called because the thrush is said to sing with greater power in stormy weather)

stounded *adj.* (also **stound**) astonished, astounded, confounded, stunned. 'I was *stounded* by what he said'

stowl *n.* a tree stump (ROWLSTONE)

straddling *v.*, *adj.* akin to loitering with intent; behaving badly. A term of dislike or contempt. 'He's been out late, *straddling* again'

strakes *n.* blacksmith's nails used in fixing iron pieces onto waggon wheels (BRAMPTON BRYAN)

strike *n.* 1. a measure holding about one peck (a unit of volume, roughly 16 pints); 2. a straight-edged piece of wood serving to flatten off a measure of grain so that it is not over-full. See *struck bushel*

stringing *v.* 1. fixing the long strings for the hops to grow up in a *hopyard*; 2. removing the stalks or stringy sides of e.g. beans

strip *v.* the phrase 'to *strip* the cows' means to take the last of the milk from them

stripe *n.* a strip (of ground or land)

stroddle *v.* to straddle, to be astride of

stroke *n.* one pass of an implement, as in ploughing the turning of one furrow. A double-pass, out and back again, is a *bout*

strong *adj.* having an offensive taste or smell; to be on the verge of going bad

struck all of a yup *adj.* (also **struck all of a heap**) too amazed to move or speak, flabbergasted (ROSS, AYLTON)

struck bushel *n.* of corn, exactly one bushel (8 gallons)

stub *n.*, *v.*, *adj.* 1. the stump of a tree (MON BORDER); 2. the prop at the bottom of a post; 3. to stock up; 4. to root out; 5. an ox

stubbanze's cowhouse *n.* a gaol

stuck to the ground *adj.* too lazy to go to work (W HEREFS)

stuff a bit of trouse in a glat *v.* to stop up a hole in a hedge (N HEREFS)

stump *n.* a square iron implement made of parallel bars close together, with a wooden handle, used to separate awns or *iles* of barley from the seed

stun *n.* stone

stupit *adj.* obstinate (a corruption of 'stupid')

sturshum *n.* nasturtium (plant)

suant *adv.*, *adj.* (also **suent, suently**) 1. gently, softly, sweetly; 2. smoothly, easily; movement as if greased; 3. well-fitting; 4. pleasantly desirable (rain after a drought might be described as *suent* rain) (WHITCHURCH)

successfully *adv.* excessively. 'It rained *successfully*'

suck *n.* a ploughshare (from the Welsh word *swch* = sword)

suddent *adj.*, *adv.* sudden, suddenly

sufferable *adj.* painful (ARCHENFIELD)

sugger *n.* sugar

suity *adj.* (pronounced 'shuty') regular or alike, well-suited, uniform. 'A nice *suity* crop of spuds'

sumber *n.* summer

summat *pron.*, *n.* (also **summut**) 1. something or other; 2. a thrashing. 'I'll give you *summut*' (N HEREFS)

summat-a-that something of that sort; something like that

sump *v.* to push along a heavy weight (KENTCHURCH)

sup *n.*, *v.* 1. a small quantity (of drink); a sip ('give us a *sup* of cider'); 2. to swallow ('to *sup* it down'); 3. to have or supply with supper; 4. a farming term meaning to give the horses their last feed of the day ('I'll *sup* the horses by nightfall')

suppose *v.* 1. to know definitely; to be certain about. 'I *suppose* I'll be there at exactly midday'; 2. assurance required of a supposition. 'He's not back till Friday, I *suppose*?'

surbated *adj.* foot-sore. 'He was weary and *surbated*'

sure-lie *adv.* surely, certainly

surry *n.* 1. a young man (a familiar form of address) (WIGMORE); 2. a strong, brawny man

swag-bellied *adj.* having a loose, prominent belly

swale *v.* to split down or off. When the bough of a tree is sawn through, if the bough gives way before being cut through, thus tearing off bark etc., this is described as '*swaling* off' or '*swaling* down'

swapson *adj.*, *n.* 1. sprawling; an expanse. 'A great *swapson* of meadow'; 2. a bad woman

sward *n.* bacon rind; the skin of a (dead) pig

swarm *v.* climb up

sway *n.* a moveable iron arm on which to suspend pots or a kettle over a cottage fire

swealing *v.*, *adj.* the guttering of a candle in a draught

sweethearts *n.* the burrs of cleavers or goosegrass (GOLDEN VALLEY)

swep *v.* past tense of the verb 'to sweep'. 'He *swep* the stable out yesterday'

swill *v.*, *n.* 1. to wash away (e.g. rain washing away soil is '*swilling* the fields'); 2. soil or mud washed off the fields by rain (LLANGARRON); 3. to flush out a ditch or a barrel

swillick *v.* to swill about. A *costrel* should never be only half-filled or the cider will *swillick* and be undrinkable

swinge *v.* to singe
swingel *n.* the shorter part (the striking *pelt*) of a flail
swipe your horn akin to 'hurry up and finish your drink'. The phrase arises from the custom in the harvest-field of workmen drinking cider from the same horn (or tot), the implication being that the drinker should pour out the dregs (*swipes*) so the next man could take his turn
swole *v.* the past tense of the verb 'to swell' (ROSS)

T

tabard *n.* stomach. Well-fed pigs are described as having their *tabards* full (from the French *tabarde* = a short coat)
tack *n., adj.* 1. hired pasture for grazing cattle ('to *tack*' = to hire pasture for cattle); 2. 'poor *tack*' = worthless stuff, of little or no use or value (NW HEREFS); 'Poor *tack*' can also mean tasteless, of poor quality, referring specifically to food or drink ('its poor *tack* and I'm not eating it'); 3. taste, spoken of cider when it has some particular taste about it ('that stuff's got a funny *tack*') (ORLETON); 4. waterlogged timber at the bottom of a river, lake etc. (if a net catches on timber below the surface, it is said to be *tacked*); 5. a harness
tag *v.* to make brown; the effect of high winds and rain on hops. 'Days of rain have *tagged* the hops' (AYLTON)
tagged *adj.* out of condition, as a horse; unhealthy-looking. 'He's *tagged* and wants exercising' (TRETIRE)
tagraling *v., adj.* 1. courting; 2. abusing
tail cratch *n.* the rack at the back of a waggon for holding hay etc.

tail wheat *n.* (also **tail corn**) small, second-rate grains used as food for poultry; poultry food. *Tail corn* is the lightest part of the corn, most easily blown away

take on *v.* 1. to take on a farm tenancy. In some areas farmers *took on* at Candlemas (2 February); in others on Lady Day (25 March); 2. to make a fuss. 'Don't *take on* so!'; 3. to pretend or feign (AYLTON)

take to *adj.*, *v.* 1. amazed, taken aback. 'She was *took to*'; 2. to rent or hire, specifically a house or land. See *set*

taken *v.* used instead of 'took'. 'I *taken* it away yesterday'

taking *adj.*, *n.* (also **to be in a taking**) 1. to be worried or distressed in mind; 2. to be in a bad temper; 3. a whitlow (an infection of the tip of the finger) is sometimes referred to as a *taking*; also, more generally, a swelling on the body not visibly occasioned by external injury; 4. an attack of sickness

tallat *n.* (also **tallant, tallard, tallet, tollard, tollet, tallit**) a loft, attic; a hayloft

tally *n.* (also **tally-stick**) e.g. during hop-picking, a piece of wood split lengthways, on which accounts were kept by notching or scoring across both halves, so that both *tally-man* and hop-picker would have a matching record of the number of bushels picked

tally-man *n.* during hop-picking, the man responsible for keeping a tally of the number of bushels of hops picked by each hop-picker. See *tally*

tamp *v.*, *adj.* 1. to go very fast (WHITCHURCH); 2. to get angry; to be in a state of readiness to release one's anger. 'I could see he was *tamping*'

tang *v.* 'To *tang* a swarm of bees' is to follow the swarm, beating loudly on a pan, a piece of metal or anything else that will give a loud ringing sound. This was reputed to induce the swarm to settle. 'At the time of swarming it is usual for the owner to tang his bees. This performance is supposed to confer upon the owner a right to follow them should they migrate. "I could follow them," said an Ashperton man lately, "even if they went into the Queen's drawing room." But if this noise be not made the claim of the loser is not admitted by others on their own premises. This old practice is rapidly passing away.' (FH)

tansel *v.* (also **tancel**) to beat, chastise, punish (ROSS)

tansilooning *v.* beating

tantadlins *n.* apple dumplings

tap *v.* to *tap* a shoe is to renew its sole. 'A *heel-tap* was a small piece of leather fixed by pegs to the end of a high-heeled shoe. Hence the figurative expression "to clear away *heel-taps*" applied to drinking the wine remaining in a glass, as being the small layer at the bottom' (GCL)

taplash *n.* bad small beer; poor quality beer

tare *adj.* eager. 'See how *tare* he is to get home!'

tater *n.*, *v.* a potato; to dig up potatoes

taunt *v.* to beg for

tay *n.* tea

tea-kettle-broth *n.* bread soaked in water and flavoured with pepper, salt and a little margarine; 'poor man's bread-and-milk'

teal *v.* (also **teel**) to prop something up against a wall; to prop a poker in front of the fire

tear to mammocks *v.* to tear to pieces

teart *adj.* (also **tiert, chiert**) 1. sore, painful, smarting. Refers especially to a sudden pain due to injury. Not often heard alone, but generally as 'a bit *tiert*'; 'middling *tiert*' etc.; 2. tart or acid (to the taste); 3. sharp ('a *tiert* frost')

teater *adj.* unsteady, wobbly, tottering. 'It was *teater*, then fell off and smashed'

ted *v.* to toss and spread new mown grass for hay (thus 'tedder' for the mechanical implement that does this)

teddies *n.* badgers (MON BORDER)

teg *n.* a one-year-old lamb

temper *n.* constitution (E HEREFS). 'She has a strong *temper*'

ten times no better *adj., adv.* rather worse in fact

t'ent *v.* it is not. '*T'ent* what he wants'

terminated *adj.* (also **termined**) determined (ROSS)

terrify *v.* to irritate (as of flies) (N HEREFS); to torment

thataway *adj.* over there. 'She left it *thataway*'

that's all about it that's the very point in question

thave *n.* a female sheep in her second year, which has ceased to lamb

the *pron.* 1. used before the names of diseases or illnesses ('*the* toothache, *the* rheumatics' etc.); 2. used before the names of trades, especially at the time of learning the trade ('he's been put to *the* butchering'; 'she's doing great at *the* dressmaking'); 3. used before the names of certain festivals ('She'll be spending *the* Christmas at home'); 4. used in place of the demonstrative pronoun 'this'

themen *pron.* those (noted by WL as still being in use in the 1970s by old country folk in W HEREFS)

thern *adj.* (also **theirn**) theirs

these *pron.* this. 'Take a look at *these* tractor'

thesen *pron.* (also **thesun**) these

they *adj.* (also **they there**) those, these. 'Pass us *they there*'

they'm *v.* they are, they have (N HEREFS)

thickun for this one or that one (CANON PYON)

thiller *n.* the shaft-horse in a team

thin *adj.* cold (of the weather) (ROSS)

things and that there a variety of things (S & W HEREFS)

think me on it *v.* remind me of it

think on *v.* to remember

this ere (also **this yer**) this. The phrase does not derive from 'this here', but from the Anglo-Saxon word *thesera* = this

thistle-finch *n.* goldfinch (bird)

thonk *n.* thong, strap, leather thing. Specifically the link or *capling* in a flail, linking the hand-shaft to the *pelt* or *swingel*. 'Two sticks and a *thonk*' = a flail

thrape *v.* 1. to thrash or beat; 2. to thresh (KINGSLAND); 3. to kill small birds (N HEREFS)

thrave *n.* (also **drave**) two dozen. A *thrave* of *boltings* = 24 *boltings* (bundles) of straw

three half-years *n.* a unit of 18 months, used to describe the age of cattle

three ha'pence *adj.* a bit simple. 'A *three ha'pence* fellow'. See *simony* and *sawney*

three singles *n.* three horses working in line ahead are described as 'driven *three singles*'

threshel *n.* (also **threshal, thresher, dreshel**) a flail (N & W HEREFS)

thripples *n.* (also **dripples, ripples**) removable extensions or rails (fore and aft) to a waggon or dray, enabling the carriage of greater loads of light, bulky material such as hay. Usually consists of three cross-members, thus *thripples* from 'three poles'

throstle *n.* (also **thrussel, thrustle**) song thrush (N HEREFS)

throwing the reed said of a cow, suffering from a prolapse of the womb

thunder and lightening *n.* Herb Robert (plant) (MARDEN)

thunder berries *n.* the large, heavy drops that fall during a thunder storm

thurn *adj., n.* 1. theirs (W HEREFS); 2. thorn

tice *v.* to entice

tid *adj.* 1. forward, skittish, playful ('a *tid* girl' = a playful girl; 'a *tid* horse' = a restive horse) (ROSS, PIXLEY); 2. of poor quality ('a *tid* lot' = not worth much)

tiddle *v.* 1. to urge on gently, to entice or induce (ROSS); to coax to eat; 2. to make much of; to fondle or pet; to nurse; 3. to kick gently (a ball etc.)

tiddled *adj.* mollycoddled

tiddling *adj., n.* (also **tidling, tidly**) a *tiddling* lamb is one brought up on the bottle (a cade lamb); a young animal nursed by hand (also a pet) might be described as a *tidler*

tidy *adj.* 'A *tidy* person' = 1. a decent, respectable person; 2. a well-to-do person; 3. a healthy person; 4. an honest or well-disposed person

tilled *v., adj.* '*Tilled* up' = propped or set up (e.g. a ladder). 'The ladder's *tilled* up, ready for the roofers'

tilter *adj.* variant of tilt or tilted. 'A *tilter* table'

tilth *n.* 1. a freshly-turned furrow; 2. the state of the land for cultivation. 'That field looks in good *tilth*'

Tim Sarah *n.* (also **tomsarah**) a sledge making contact with the ground in front, and having wheels behind; a light gambo or cart. The word probably derives from the Welsh *tim* + *saerni* = little + wright's work or joinery (W HEREFS)

timber tree *n.* a large tree intended for felling and from which e.g. planks might be cut (MON BORDER)

timbersome *adj.* timorous, shy

time a gone *n.* time passed

timmy *adj.* timid, irritable

tine *v., n.* 1. to mend a *glat* or bind up a hedge; 2. a prong. 'The *tine* of a *pikle*'; the tooth of a harrow

ting-tang *n.* the small bell sounded before the start of a church service, after the 'peal' has ended

tinna *v.* it is not. '*Tinna* nice weather out there'

tinnen *adj.* made of tin (as 'wooden' for made of wood)

tinnet *n.* (also **tinnet, tinnit, tinth tynnet**) brushwood used in mending a gap or *glat* in a hedge (N HEREFS)

tired *adj.* retired (S HEREFS)

tishiebobbie *n.* a thumb-sucking child. 'Bless the little *tishiebobbie*' (BROMSASH, UPTON BISHOP)

tissock *n., v.* (also **tissick, tissuck, tussock**) a cough; to cough (N HEREFS) (from the French *tousser* = to cough)

tissocky *adj.* (also **tissicky, tussicky, tussocky**) asthmatical, chesty (*tussocking* for a hard, dry cough) (ARCHENFIELD)

tisty-tosty *n.* a cowslip ball; a nosegay made of cowslips (from the Middle English *tyte tust*)

titlark *n.* used for both the tree and meadow pipit (birds)

titter *n.*, *v.* (also **titter-totter**) 1. a see-saw; 2. to sway slightly on one's feet; to totter; 3. to be shaken up and down, as the bough of a tree. Also appears in place-names (*Titter*stone, *Totter*hill etc.); *tittering* = swinging (SUTTON ST NICHOLAS)

titter wren *n.* wren (bird)

titty whitethroat *n.* whitethroat (bird). *Titty* is a prefix that may be applied to any warbler (ROWLSTONE)

to *adv.* almost. 'He is *to* seventy but doesn't look it'

to-broke *adj.* broken in pieces (WHITCHURCH)

to-year *adv.* in this year. Used like 'today', 'tonight' etc.

toady *adj.*, *n.* hateful; a loathsome person

toby *n.* fox; Reynard the Fox (KINGSTONE)

tod *n.* 1. an oddment, e.g. of a small package among larger. 100 bags of corn of full measure plus one small one = 100 bags and a *tod*; 2. a *tod* of 28lbs is a unit of weight used by wool-staplers, roughly equivalent to four fleeces

tolt *v.* told

tomahawk *n.* mattock

tommy *n.* (pronounced 'tummy') food, lunch

tongue fern *n.* hart's tongue fern

took *v.* (also **tuck**) past participle of the verb 'to take'

top *n.* ground ploughed such that two furrows fall together to form a *top*

top and bottom of the matter *n.* the point (of the matter) (MON BORDER). *High top and bottom of the matter* is used in the GOLDEN VALLEY

top up *v.* to finish a hayrick at the top

tope *n.* bullfinch (bird)
tops *n.* term of endearment applied to children ('little *tops*')
toro *n.* (also **tauro**) bull (MUCH COWARNE)
torrel *n.* (also **torrell**) fool or simpleton; a twit (LEDBURY); a term with an abusive or offensive implication used in a jocular manner, as a form of address ('You old *torrel!*')
tossetty *adj.* old and decrepit; needing much attention due to age and infirmity. 'She's seventy and getting *tossetty*'
tosticated *adj.* 1. intoxicated (LEOMINSTER); puzzled or confused; 2. tossed about, disturbed in the mind
tot *n.* 1. drinking horn; 2. a small cup; 3. a small drink
t'others *n.* commonly used for 'the others'
totteries *n.* part of the ploughing gear when horses are used
tow *n.* the refuse of flax (linseed). See *herds*
towardly *adj.* (pronounced as per 'cowardly') 1. docile, well-behaved, compliant. The opposite of *frowardly* or *untowardly.* 'The old cow came along as *towardly* as a daisy' (BRIDSTOW); 2. prosperous, doing well
towtree *n.* horse chestnut tree
traffic *n.* a track or passage made by rats or game
tram *n.*, *v.* (also **tramming**) 1. a wooden frame to support a cask; 2. 'To *tram* the beer' = to place a cask on the *tram* in order to tap it
trampsey *adj.* slushy underfoot. 'It's getting *trampsey* out'
tranch *n.* area of woodland allotted for felling (from the French *trancher* = to cut, slice)
transalooning *n.*, *v.* a good walloping
translator *n.* cobbler
tree *n.* handle, e.g. of a spade. 'The *tree* of a *spittle*'

tremenduous *adj.* tremendous
trig *n.* a gutter or small ditch (N HEREFS)
trig out *v.* to mark out, as defining boundaries
t'right go to the right. See Waggoner's calls, p. 178
trim *v.* to scold
trimple *v.* to tread gingerly or uncomfortably
trin *n.* a flat tub for receiving cider from a press
trinding *v.* winding wool to supply to a draper's
trolly *n.* a low, four-wheeled waggon without sides; a sledge used in husbandry, for transporting e.g. an injured sheep
trough *n.* ('ou' pronounced as in 'dough') a water trough (MON BORDER)
trouse *n.* (also **trowse**) brushwood, trimmings from hedges or trees, sometimes used to fill *glats* (N & W HEREFS)
trow *n.* a trough, as in a pig-*trow*, pump-*trow* etc.
trowing *n.* ('ow' pronounced as in 'throw') roof gutter (MON BORDER)
truckle off *v.* to move away; to go off
truss *n.* a measure of weight for hay or straw
try *n.* a wire screen for cleansing wheat from chaff
tuffet *n.* (also **tuft**) a heap of grass (LLANGARRON)
tug mutton *n.* broad-leaved plantain (plant)
tugers *n.* rods (hazel) used in thatching (KENTCHURCH)
tullock *n.* a hillock
tump *n.*, *v.* 1. a small rounded hill; 2. an ant or mole hill. See *oontitump*; 3. a stack or *bury* in which root vegetables (e.g. for fodder) are kept through the winter; 4. a heap of anything; 5. to put potatoes and other roots in a *tump*. From the Welsh verb *twmp* = to put into small heaps

tundish *n.* (also **tun-dish**) a wooden funnel for pouring beer or cider into a flask

tunning dish *n.* a wooden dish used in dairies and brewing

turmits *n.* (also **mips, mits, nips**) turnips

turn *n.* to 'get the *turn*' is to pass the point of crisis, to show signs of improvement. 'She's got the *turn* on it now'

turn the head *v.* to tend in sickness. 'My mother is ill, and needs a nurse to *turn the head* of her'

turnip-chat *n.* (also **turnip-hoe**) a fork with one side square to hoe up and the other V-shaped to pull out

turtle-doo *n.* turtle-dove (bird)

tush *v.* to drag or push with difficulty, without the use of mechanical aids (wheels, skids etc.); specifically refers to the hauling of timber, or dragging of wood. 'Go and *tush* those felled branches'. *Tushing* = hauling

tussicated *adj.* tormented

tussing and snessing *v.* coughing and sneezing

tut *n.* (also **tit**) a projection (usually small), for example a lever or drawer handle. See *nub*

twaddle *n.* (also **dwaddle**) nonsense, idle chatter, gossip (*twattle* is recorded in LEOMINSTER)

twang *n.* dialect; accent (LEOMINSTER)

twash *n.* nonsense, rubbish (ROSS)

twerten *v.* stir up. 'Get a stick and *twerten* it up a bit'

tweselty *adj.* poor looking

twichild *adj.* doting

twil *n.* a tell-tale, sneak (WIGMORE)

twink *n.* (also **pink**) chaffinch (from the sound of its call)

twirty *adj.* saucy

twitch *v.* to touch

twivelling *v.* ploughing for the first time (TRETIRE)

twlth *n.* 1. a hollow; 2. occasionally a pleat (W HEREFS)

two-sticks-and-a-thonk *n.* a flail (*thonk* refers not to the sound it makes, but the link or *capling* between the sticks)

two words for one *v.* getting the worst of it in an argument. 'I wound him up and got *two words for one*'

twy-bill *n.* (also **twybill**) a tool like a pick axe, cutting two ways with ends three inches broad: one cuts in a line with the handle, the other at right-angles to it (ASHPERTON)

twy-fallow *v.* cross-ploughing (ploughing in one direction, then again at 90 degrees to the existing furrows)

tyndton *n.* a place bound up, fenced in (ARCHENFIELD)

U

ucking *n.*, *v.* (also **hucking**) 1. an amount of ploughing done in a given time (WIGMORE); 2. 'A good *ucking*' = a good load (e.g. of hay) (LINGEN)

ulster throat *n.* an ulcerated throat (N HEREFS)

'ummock *n.* hillock, mound of earth

un *pron.* 1. him; it. 'Hit *un* hard!'; 2. used instead of 'in' at the start of words (e.g. 'indecent' becomes *un*decent etc.)

unaccountable *adv.* (the first syllable pronounced 'on') extremely, very, uncommonly, surprisingly

unaccountables *n.* used in the phrase 'God Almighty's *unaccountables*', meaning those who are somewhat too clever (LEOMINSTER)

uncommon *adv.* (also **oncommon**) very much, exceedingly

undeniable *adj.* excellent, good

underminded *adj.* devious; a portmanteau word combining 'underhand' and 'evil-minded' (ARCHENFIELD)

unforbidden *adj.* (also **unforbiddenest**) wilful, unruly. 'A most *unforbiddenest ronkest* young rascal' (LEOMINSTER)

ungainly *adj.* unhandy, inconvenient

unhonest *adj.* dishonest

unket *adj.* (also **unkert, unkut, unkit**) 1. awkward, lacking in manners; 2. lonely, solitary; 3. unfavourable (weather)

unkind *adj.* 1. unthrifty, not doing well (animals and plants); 2. bad, unfavourable for crops etc. (weather)

unlucky *adj.* troublesome, mischievous (N HEREFS)

unproper *adj.* improper, indecent

unsuity *adj.* unequal, irregular. See *suity*

unt *n.* (also **oont, woont**) ('u' pronounced as in 'pudding') mole (from the Old English *wand*). See *oont*

untidy *adj.* dishonest ('an *untidy* trick' = a shameful action)

untitump *n.* (also **unty-tump, oontitump**) molehill

untowardly *adj.* badly behaved

up *v.* to rise with vigour and anger. 'I *upped* and told him what I thought of him'

up-hill *adj.*, *adv.* north, especially applied to the wind

up in one's sitting sitting up in one's bed

upon *adv.* (also **upon times**) sometimes, occasionally, now and then. 'He do get drunk *upon times*' (S & W HEREFS)

upperter *adj.* taller, as of women. 'She was *upperter* than her sister' (CANON PYON)

uprit *adj.* upright, proud

uproar *n.* disorder, confusion, but not necessarily involving noise. 'The garden is all in an *uproar* with weeds'

upsides *adv.* 'to get *upsides* with' = to get even with; to get one's own back; tit for tat

urched *adj.* (also **nurped, ooched**) huddled up (with cold) (LEDBURY, LEOMINSTER)

urchin *n.* 1. a hedgehog; 2. a dirty child

urts *n.* fragments left over, generally used to refer to corn, chaff etc., left uneaten in a horse's manger

utas *n.* a quarrel (rare). See *kelute*

uv *prep.* with. 'I've been up the dingle *uv* the dog'

uvvermost *adj., adv.* uppermost

V

vails *n.* a perquisite, fee or tip, specifically payable to a man hired as a cowherd when he took a cow from home

vally *n.* 1. value; 2. the felloe (rim) of a wheel; 3. a litter of pigs (CLODOCK)

vantage nib *n.* of a scythe, the lower of the two *nibs*, usually cranked and held in the right hand

vapouring about *v.* engaged in aimless actions or talk

varges *n.* crab vinegar (from crab apples). Traditionally found only in the expression 'as sour as *varges*'

veerings *n.* ploughed land is said to be laid out into broad *veerings* when numerous furrows are turned up on each side against the same ridge

veldy bird *n.* fieldfare (bird)

venur'some *adj.* adventurous

vern *n.* (also **vearn**) 1. fern; 2. a partner in a mine, in the Forest of Dean (probably from the Anglo-Saxon *fera* or *gefera* = a partner, companion)

very middling *adj.* very ill

vessel *n.* cider cask

vindicative *adj.* vindictive (ROSS)

vitrous *adj.* inveterate, bitter, implacable

void *adj.* empty, referring specifically to a house (N HEREFS, KINGSTONE)

volk *n.* folk. 'Oomen *volk*' = women

vool *n.* fool. 'An oal *vool*'

vor *prep.* 1. for; 2. four (numeral)

vor wy for why; the reason. 'I'll tell you *vor wy*'

vorty *n.* forty

W

wad *n.* 1. a small heap of haycock in a hay field; 2. a burden. 'Rid me of this *wad*'

wag *v.* (also **waggin'**) 1. to move, stir; moving; 2. 'He's not *waggin'* it right' = he's not doing it properly; he's not using the tool in the right way (E HEREFS)

waggoners' calls see p. 178

waggoner's rain *n.* a torrential downpour, drenching rain (MUCH MARCLE); locally defined as rain falling 'straight down or straight across'. A waggoner was expected to stay at work unless the conditions were quite impossible

wainus *n.* a wainhouse or cart-shed

waiter *n.* water

wake *n.* a parish festival, held on the first Sunday after the day of the saint to whom the church is dedicated

walker's earth *n.* (also **waler's soap**) fuller's earth (a fine clay used in the fulling of cloth, to absorb grease etc.)

wallies *n.* (also **wollies**) windrows; long ridges or rows into which hay is raked before being gathered for haycocks and being carried (UPPER SAPEY, MUCH COWARNE)

wallop *v.*, *n.* 1. to beat or thrash; 2. beer

wallowish *adj.* (also **wallowy**) 1. faint or sickly tasting; 2. nauseous (derived from to *wall*, meaning that which makes the stomach rise)

wally *n.* (also **wolly**) a ridge; a long windrow of drying hay (MUCH COWARNE)

wambling *adj.* (also **wambly, wombly**) shaky, unsteady. 'I felt a bit *wambly* like' (E HEREFS)

wame *v.*, *adj.* (also **wame about**) 1. to veer about as a weathercock; 2. also describes the gait of a drunken man

wandering Jew *n.* tradescantia (plant) (ROSS)

wane *n.*, *adj.* (also **waney**) the edge of a plank which is not rectangular, due to being cut from the side of the trunk

wankling *adj.* 1. weakly (particularly of a child) (TRETIRE); 2. tottery, insecure

waps *n.* wasp

warm *v.*, *adj.* (pronounced as in 'arm') 1. to thrash, beat. 'I'll *warm* your hide'; 2. very hot

warmship *n.* warmth. Also used in the sense of hospitality. 'They showed me great *warmship*' (TENBURY)

warned *v.* warrant. 'He is the quickest, I *warned* you'

warth *n.* a flat meadow close to a stream or river bank

wassall *v.*, *adj.* messing (spoken of fowls)

wastle *v.* to wander

watchard *adj.* literally 'wet shod' (having wet feet or shoes). 'I'm *watchard* after fording the brook'

water bewitched *adj.* applied to very weak tea or ale. 'Water *bewitched* and ale *begrudged*'

water bridge *n.* specifically a bridge over a brook or river

water-sweet *adj.* fresh and clean after washing. 'Here's your laundry, *water-sweet*' (TRETIRE)

watty handed *adj.* (also **watty-handed**) butter-fingered, clumsy, ungainly

wauve *v.* to cover over, as dishes at a table

wave *v.* to fail. 'She'll *wave* if she tries to go that way'

weaner *n.* an eight-week-old pig

weany *adj.* weakly, puny (of a child) (ARCHENFIELD)

wee weed *n.* lesser convulvulus (plant)

weed away *v.* to waste away; to become less, perhaps without anything to show for it (as of money)

welcome home the *welcome home* is the name given to the gentle chiming of the bells as the funeral procession nears the church (N HEREFS)

welcome-home-husband-though-never-so-late *n.* house-leek (plant)

welistering *adj.*, *adv.* very, extremely; used only to qualify the word 'great'. 'I caught a *welistering* great rat'

welk *adj.* withered. 'The crop's *welk* from lack of water'

well-ended *adj.* a term applied to hayricks that have been closely pulled and neatly finished

welly *adv.* well nigh; nearly, almost. 'The area of that field is *welly* six acres'

we'm *v.* we are; we have (N HEREFS)

wen *n.* a bulge or swelling

wenchen *n.* wenches

went *v.* past participle of the verb 'to go'. 'I'd 'ave like to 'ave *went*'; 'I wanted to *went*'

werrit *adj.*, *n.* (also **worrit**) 1. to be anxious, to worry; 2. one of an anxious, fidgety disposition. 'He's a bit of a *werrit*'

wesh *v.*, *n.* 1. to wash; 2. the receptacle for pig's food was commonly called 'the *wesh* tub' (TRETIRE)

wesh beetle *n.* a wooden implement, spade-shaped, used to beat wet linen on a washing block (W HEREFS)

wet-bird *n.* chaffinch (bird)

whatsomever *pron.* (also **whatsomdever**) whatever

whet *v.*, *n.* 1. to sharpen. When scything, if the scythe does not cut well, one '*whets* and tries again'; 2. also used more generally to refer to a second go at something. 'If that fails have another *whet*'

whiffeldy *adj.* (also **whiffling**) slight, light, uncertain; changeable, wavering. 'The wind's *whiffeldy* this morning'

whinders *n.* bits, pieces; used only in the expression 'to break to *whinders*' = to break to pieces

whipstitch *n.*, *adj.* 1. a quick, recurring interval. 'She's out in the fields every *whipstitch*' = as often as possible; 2. also used to describe e.g. planting in a careless, irregular manner. 'He planted the saplings *whipstitch*'

whisket *n.* (also **wisket**) 1. a gardening basket (N HEREFS); 2. a large basket without handles, used for carrying fodder to animals; 3. a round, open basket made of flat bands of wood. See *kuype*

whit *n.* (also **wit**) wheat

white bellied 'uns *n.* local description of the short-tailed vole, which has white underparts

white hen's chicken *n.* a mother's favourite. 'The oldest boy is the *white hen's chicken*' (LEOMINSTER)

whitefaced 'uns *n.* 1. Hereford cattle; 2. Herefordians

whitsun boss *n.* guelder rose

whosen *pron.* whose. '*Whosen* boots are those?'

whossuck *v.*, *n.* cough. 'Her *whossucked* and ridded wonderful' = she coughed and cleared her throat well (FH)

whul *adj.*, *n.* (pronounced 'hul') whole

whully *adv.* (pronounced 'hully') wholly

whum *n.* (also **wum**) home

wicked *adj.* 1. playful, lively (e.g. a child); 2. fierce, savage

wicken *n.* (also **wicken-tree, witan, whitley, whitty-tree, wittern, witty, witty tree**) rowan, mountain ash (tree)

wid! wid! (also **widdy! widdy!**) call to ducks. See Calls to animals, p. 177

widduck *n.* (also **wid'uck**) weed hook (WHITCHURCH)

wide side of the road 'to give one the *wide side of the road*' = to give one a wide berth; to steer clear of

wids *n.* weeds

wiff *n.* a corruption of 'weave'. A thin rod, usually of hazel, ash or willow, used to tie faggots. See *neal*

wig *n.* an old-fashioned cake or bun. 'A small, oblong roll, baked with butter and currants' (GCL). Wig cakes 'are still made at Hereford and Leominster. Formerly they were held in great repute, but are now enquired for only by old-fashioned folk. Messrs. Bomford and Lee (formerly Alcott, or Husbands), 46 Commercial Street, Hereford, make them. Also Mr. Beard, School Lane, Leominster.' (FH, writing in the 1880s)

wik *n.* week

wild *adj.* rough (used e.g. for rough, coarse-grained lumps of stone) (ORCOP)

wild hook *n.* a long-handled hook for cutting hedges

wilk-car *n.* a horse-drawn waggon (WIGMORE)

wilter *v.* to wilt, wither (MON BORDER)

wince *n.*, *v.* a variant of 'winch'

windering *adj.*, *v.* not doing well; struggling (e.g. of a failing crop). 'The wheat is *windering*'

winnow *n.*, *v.* a sound given forth by a horse when expecting or wishing for food or water

winter stuff *n.* winter greens (kale, cabbages etc.)

wires *n.* the framework of string or twine upon which hop or strawberry shoots or runners are trained

wise man *n.* a wizard; a man who works charms

wise woman *n.* a witch; a woman who works charms

wishful *adj.* 'to be *wishful*' = to want, to desire

witch *n.* a wise man or woman

witch-hole *n.* a small opening in the wall near the fireplace in which the tinder box was kept (MON BORDER)

witches' stirrups *n.* the matted locks in a horse's mane. Witches were believed to ride horses on May Eve so madly that their manes became tied in knots

witherdy *adj.* withered. 'The flowers are gone all *witherdy*'

withies *n.* (also **withs**) 1. osiers; willow cuttings for binding faggots; 2. bands cut from a rowan tree (mountain ash) for thatching or tying up faggots (ORLETON); 3. more generally, a *with* can be any twisted band of wood

without *conj.* unless. 'He won't know *without* you tell him'

withy tree *n.* willow tree
withy wool *n.* old man's beard, traveller's joy (plant)
wizzel *n.* dipper (bird). The name may be a reference to the bird's 'zit, zit' call, or from its whirring flight
wombling *adj.* awkward, clumsy. 'You great *wombling* lump'; irregular, of walking (ARCHENFIELD)
wonty-tump *n.* (pronounced 'oonty-tump') molehill. See *oontitump*
wooding *v.* (also **'ooding**) 'to go *wooding*' = to collect kindling wood (MON BORDER)
woolly bears *n.* hairy caterpillars
woont *n.* (also **want, wont, hoont**) mole. See *oont* and *unt*
woot *v.* (also **'oot**) will you. 'Pass me that fork *woot*'
wopper *n.* wasp. 'I got stung by a *wopper*'. See *waps*
word *v.* to reprove. 'I'll *word* him for what he done'
wore *adj.*, *v.* worn. 'The soles of your boots look *wore* out'
work *v.* to ferment (wine, cider etc.)
work-brittle *adj.* industrious, eager to work
work-hard-and-starve n. a facetious term among tradesmen for a bricklayer's trowel, in reference to the best-known maker, William Hunt & Sons, whose initials are W.H.S. (thus *work-hard-and-starve*)
work the sids *v.* to sow the seeds (*sids*) in (LLANGARRON)
workaday *n.* weekday. Clothes not worn on Sundays might be described as '*workaday* clothes'
worser *adj.*, *adv.* (also **wusser**) worse
worthine *n.* a quantity of land, so-called in the manor of Kingsland (where tenants were known as *worthies*)
worts *n.* whortleberries, bilberries

woser *n.* (also **wooser**) ('s' pronounced as 'z') a young pig (WIGMORE)

wound *n.* ('ou' pronounced as in 'sound') a nasty wound, an inflamed sore

woundy *adv.*, *adj.* very, exceedingly

wozzle *v.* to twist. 'Give it a *wozzle* and pull it out'

writing lark *n.* yellowhammer, named for the scribble-like markings on the bird's eggs (WHITCHURCH before the Second World War). See *scribbling schoolmaster*

writings *n.* deeds, records (S HEREFS)

wrobble *n.*, *v.* (also **robble**) 1. a confusion ('in a *wrobble*' = in confusion); 2. to wrap up

wum *n.* (also **oaum**) home

wunna *v.* won't; will not; was not

wurr *n.* hoar frost (LEDBURY)

wuth *n.* worth

wytch *n.* the body of a waggon

wyzzel *n.* the top ridge of straw in thatching a rick (KENTCHURCH)

Y

y a common prefix heard in Herefordshire, including in the pronunciation of place-names (*Yersley* = Eardisley etc.)

yaffle *n.* (also **yeckle, yekkle, yaffil**) green woodpecker

yander *adv.*, *adj.* yonder

yap *n.* heap

yar *n.* 1. hair; 2. hare

yarb *n.*, *v.* 1. an idle good-for-nothing; 2. *yarbs* = herbs; 3. to cut roughly. '*Yarb* it up and chuck it in the pot'

yarbalist *n.* herbalist

yarn *v.* 1. to earn; 2. to stare. 'Don't just stand and *yarn*'

yat *n.* gate, specifically one made of interlaced twigs (SYMOND'S YAT)

yaup *v.* (also **yowp**) 1. to yelp, particularly as a dog (ROSS); 2. to yawn loudly

yead *n.* (also **yed, yud** – pronounced 'e-ud') head

yean *v., adj.* of a ewe, to give birth; to lamb. See *ean*

yeaning *v.* lambing (WIGMORE)

years *n.* ears

yeller *n.* (also **yeller jarnders, yellot**) jaundice

yeller amber *n.* (also **yeller omber, yellow homber, yellow omber,** N HEREFS) yellowhammer (S HEREFS)

yellerbee *n.* wasp

yent? (also **yunt?**) are you not? '*Yent* ready to go yet?'

yent it? (also **yunt it?**) is it not?

yep *n.* a heap. *Unt-yep* = molehill

yet *v.* (also **yut**) to eat. '*Yet* it all up'

yimp *n.* a small twig. 'Windfall *yimps* carpet the orchard' (W HEREFS)

yocksing *v.* heaving of the stomach (SUTTON ST NICHOLAS)

yon *pron., adv., adj.* 1. that; 2. yonder

yonk *v.* to skulk; to sneak off (as a fox). 'He snatched a hen and *yonked* off sharpish'

yop *n.* nape. 'He got the dog by the *yop* of his neck'

yorrocks *n.* the straps tied by a farm labourer around the knees of his trousers

yourn *pron.* (also **yurn**) yours

yow *n.* (also **yoe, yowe**) ewe

yuckle *n*. green woodpecker
yum *n*. home. 'Get yourself off *yum*'
yumbuck *n*. hymn book. 'Open your *yumbucks*'
yup *n*. 1. a large quantity (as a heap of soil); 2. 'To be struck all of a *yup*' = to be overcome with astonishment

Z

zeedum *v*. saw them. 'I *zeedum* coming' (N HEREFS)
zick! a waggoner's call to turn right (NW HEREFS). See Waggoners' calls, p. 178
zulu *n*. a plaited straw hat used by workmen, now extinct
zummut *n*., *pron*., *adv*. something

~

Local names of birds in Herefordshire

from Henry Graves Bull, *Notes on the Birds of Herefordshire*, 1888

Screech Owl, White Owl Barn Owl
Merle, Ouzel Blackbird
Reed Sparrow, Water Sparrow Black-headed Bunting
Bluecap, Tom Tit, Willow Biter Blue Tit
Bud Bird, Budding Bird, Cock Hoop, Hoop, Hoof, Hope, Tope Bullfinch
Pink, Pinkin, Pyefinch, Pyerinch, Shelly, Twink, Wet-bird Chaffinch
Cushat, Queest, Quist, Wood-pigeon Collared Dove
Bald Coot Coot
Shell-apple Crossbill
Water Blackbird, Water Ouzel, White-throated Blackbird, Wizzel Dipper
Blue Rump, Blue Tail, Felt, Feltyfare, Veldebird Fieldfare
Gold Linnet, Seven-coloured Linnet, Thistle-finch Goldfinch
Gull (*pl.* Gullets), Goosmachick Gosling
Blackcap, Oxeye Great Tit
Green Linnet Greenfinch
Hickle, Rain-bird, Stock-heckle, Storm-bird, Yaffil, Yuckle Green Woodpecker
Aizack, Blue Isaac Hedge Sparrow

Crane, Hern Heron
Spadger House Sparrow
Green Plover, Peewit Lapwing
Dabchick, Didapper, Divvy Duck Little Grebe
Bottle Tit, Canbottle, Mummiruffin, Mumruffin, Ragamuffin Long-tailed Tit
Madge, Magot, Pie Magpie
Holly Thrush, Holme Screech, Mistletoe Thrush, Storm Cock, Storm Screech Missel (Mistle) Thrush
Churn-owl, Fern-owl, Goat Sucker, Night Churr Nightjar
Jelly Hooter, Oolat Owl
Butcher Bird, Flusher Red-backed Shrike
Brantail, Branter, Kitty Brantail, Fire-brand Tail Redstart
Summer Snipe Sandpiper
Ground Lark Skylark
Mavis, Throstle Song Thrush
Blue Hawk Sparrow Hawk
Beam Bird Spotted Flycatcher
Black Steer, Sheep-stare, Stare Starling
Gorse Bird Stonechat
Devilin, Skeer, Skir-devil, Squeaker Swift
Brown Owl, Wood Owl Tawny Owl
Titlark Tree & Meadow Pipit
Water Wagtail Wagtail
Furze-chat, Haytick Whinchat
Haybird, Nettle Creeper, Titty Whitethroat Whitethroat
Nettle-bird, Willow Wren, Yellow Wren Willow Warbler
Kitty Wren Wren
Cuckoo's Mate, Snake Bird Wryneck
Ammer, Writing Lark, Yellow Bunting, Yellowhomber Yellowhammer

Calls to animals

baa! baa-ho! baa! call to sheep
birdie! birdie! call to guinea fowl
chick! chick! (also **chook! chook!**) call to hens
chig! chig! call to pigs
coop! coop! (also **koop! koop!**) call to horses
dilly! dilly! dilly! (also **dil! dil!**) call to geese
ey-ah! ey-ah boy! call to one's dog
ho! ho! ho! (also **hoop! hoop!**) call for driving loose cattle
hoi! hoi! hoi! (also **hi! hi!**, **hip! hi!** in Worcestershire) call for driving loose sheep
kerp! kerp! (also **kepp! kepp!**) call to poultry in general
poi! poi! poi! call to cattle
purr! purr! call to turkeys
sieu! sieu! sieu! ('*sieu*' to rhyme with 'stew') (also **diou! diou!**, **si-ew! si-ew!**; **stew pig!**, **stew Jack!**, **stoo!**) call for driving loose pigs
wid! wid! (also **widdy! widdy!**) call to ducks

Waggoners' calls

aet! go to the right (NE HEREFS)
aya! to the near side; come over (to a team of horses) (E HEREFS)
come here back! (also **c'mere, c'mere a bit, come 'ere back**) turn left (E HEREFS)
ease aya fust! move forward (E HEREFS)
gee! gee-back! turn right (E HEREFS)
haw! go left (NE HEREFS)
hoot! turn right
oot! to the offside (to a team of horses) (E HEREFS)
see! see back! turn right
stand back! come back (E HEREFS)
t'right! go to the right
zick! turn right (NW HEREFS)

BIBLIOGRAPHY

A.F. Parkes & Co. catalogue, No. N25 (local tools and farm implements), ND (TATHS LIBRARY* NO. 3854)

Bannister, Revd A.T., *The Place-Names of Herefordshire, their origin and development*, privately printed for the author at Cambridge University Press, 1916

Boucher, Jonathan, *A Glossary of Obsolete and Provincial Words Forming a Supplement to the Dictionaries of the English Language*, Black, Young & Young, 1833

Britten, James, *Old Country and Farming Words: Gleaned from Agricultural Books*, Trübner & Co. for The English Dialect Society, 1880

Britten, James & Holland, Robert, *A Dictionary of English Plant Names*, Trübner & Co. for The English Dialect Society, 1878

Bull, Henry Graves, *Some Notes on the Birds of Herefordshire*, Jakeman and Carver, 1888

Chamberlain, Edith, *Glossary of West Worcestershire Words*, English Dialect Society No. 36, Trübner & Co., 1882

Coplestone-Crow, Bruce, *Herefordshire Place-names*, Logaston Press, 2009

* held at the Museum of English Rural Life in Reading

Crystal, David, *The Cambridge Encyclopedia of the English Language* (3rd edn), Cambridge University Press, 2018
—, *The Disappearing Dictionary: A Treasury of Lost English Dialect Words*, Macmillan, 2015
Drummond Robertson, J., *A Glossary of Dialect and Archaic Words used in the County of Gloucester*, English Dialect Society, Kegan Paul, Trench, Trübner & Co., 1890
Duncumb, John, *Collections towards the History and Antiquity of the County of Hereford*, E.G. Wright, 1804
Grigson, Geoffrey, *The Englishman's Flora*, Phoenix House Ltd, 1955
Grose, Francis, *A Glossary of Provincial and Local Words used in England*, John Russell Smith, 1839
Haggard, Andrew, *Dialect and Local Usages of Herefordshire*, Grower Books, 1972
Halliwell, J.O., *Dictionary of Archaic and Provincial Words* (2 Vols), J.R. Smith, 1847
Havergal, Francis Tebbs, *Herefordshire Words and Phrases*, W. Henry Robinson, 1887
Hughes, Anne, *Her Boke*, The Folio Society, 1981
Huntley, Revd R.W., *Glossary of Cotswold Dialect: Illustrated by Examples from Ancient Authors*, Russell Smith, 1868
Hywel Wyn, Owen & Morgan, Richard, *Dictionary of the Place-Names of Wales*, Gomer, 2007
Jackson, Georgina F., *Shropshire Word-Book, A Glossary of Provincial Words etc. used in the County*, Trübner & Co., 1879
James, Isaac & John Fussell catalogue (local tools and farm implements), *c.*1885 (reprinted by the Tools & Trades History Society in 2001, TATHS LIBRARY NO. 2829)
John Wooldridge & Sons catalogue (local tools and farm implements), 1906 (TATHS LIBRARY NO. 3861)

Lawson, Revd R., *Upton-on-Severn Words and Phrases*, English Dialect Society No. 42, Trübner & Co., 1884
Leather, Ella Mary, *The Folk-Lore of Herefordshire*, Logaston Press, 2018 (first published 1912 by Jakeman and Carver)
Leeds, Winifred, *Herefordshire Speech*, privately published (Ross-on-Wye), 1974
Lewis, George Cornewall, *A Glossary of Provincial Words used in Herefordshire*, John Murray, 1839
Macfarlane, Robert, *Landmarks*, Penguin Books, 2015
Malden, Walter J., *Tillage and Implements* (Bell's Agricultural Series), George Bell & Sons, 1891
Morgan, W.E.T., *Radnorshire Words*, English Dialect Society, Trübner & Co., 1881
Nares, Archdeacon Robert, *A Glossary, or Collection of Words, Phrases, Names, and Allusions to Customs, Proverbs etc.*, Reeves and Turner, 1888 (first published 1790)
Northall, G.F., *Folk-phrases of Four Counties (Gloucestershire, Staffordshire, Warwickshire, Worcestershire)*, English Dialect Society, Henry Frowde, 1894
Orton, H. et al, *Survey of English Dialects: The Basic Material* (4 Vols), E.J. Arnold & Sons Ltd, 1962–71
—, *The Linguistic Atlas of England*, Croom Helm, 1978
— & Wright, N., *A Word Geography of England*, Seminar Press, 1975
Philips, John, *Cyder. A Poem. In Two Books*, H. Hills (Black-Fryars, near the Water-side), 1709
Porson, Revd A., *Notes of quaint Words and Sayings in the dialect of South Worcestershire*, James Parker & Co., 1875
Potter, Stephen & Sargent, Laurens, *Pedigree: Essays on the Etymology of Words from Nature* (The New Naturalist Series No. 56), Collins, 1973

Purchas, William Henry & Ley, Augustin, *A Flora of Herefordshire*, Jakeman and Carver, 1889

Ray, John & Bohn, Henry George, *A Collection of English Words not Generally Used*, W. Otridge et al, 1768

Salisbury, Jesse, *A Glossary of Words and Phrases used in S. E. Worcestershire*, English Dialect Society No. 72, Trübner & Co., 1893

Smythe Palmer, Revd A., *Folk-Etymology. A Dictionary of Verbal Corruptions or Words Perverted in Form or Meaning, by False Derivation or Mistaken Analogy*, George Bell and Sons, 1882

Swainson, Revd Charles, *Provincial Names and Folk Lore of British Birds*, Trübner & Co. for The English Dialect Society, 1885

Trudgill, Peter, *The Dialects of England* (2nd edn.), Blackwell Publishing, 2003

Waters, Ivor, *Folklore & Dialect of the Lower Wye Valley*, The Chepstow Society, 1973

Wright, Joseph, *The English Dialect Dictionary* (6 Vols), Henry Frowde, 1905 (this has been digitised, and is available online at: www.eddonline4-proj.uibk.ac.at/edd/)

Wright, Thomas, *Dictionary of Obsolete and Provincial Words*, Bohn, 1857

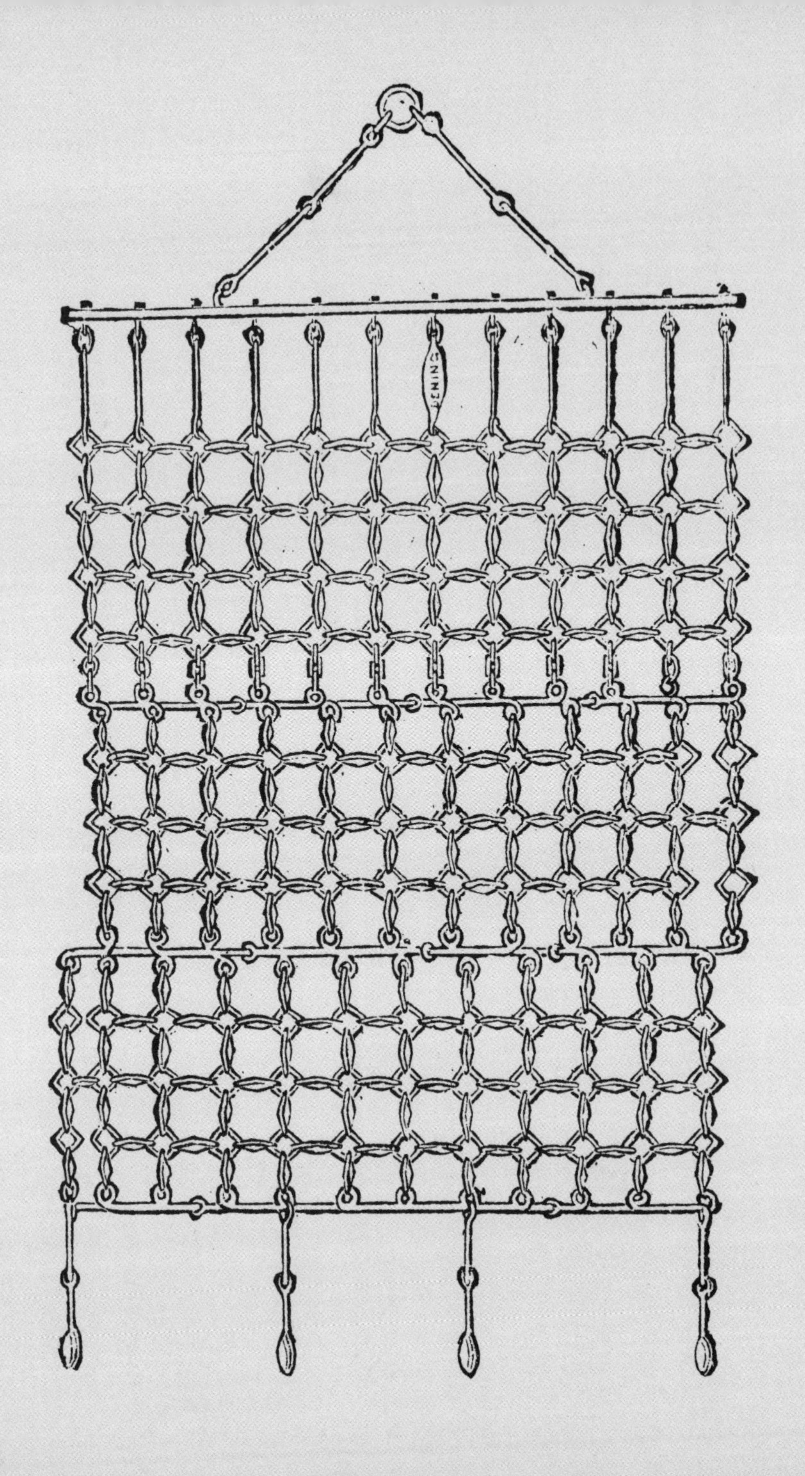